MW00789861

CHANGE

is

POSSIBLE

CHANGE
is
POSSIBLE
I Never Gave Up

a memoir

EDDIE ELLIS

atmosphere press

© 2023 Eddie Ellis

Published by Atmosphere Press

Cover design by Matthew Fielder

This book is a memoir. It reflects the author's present recollections of experiences over time. Some names and characteristics have been changed, some events have been compressed, and some dialogue has been recreated.

No part of this book may be reproduced without permission from the author except in brief quotations and in reviews.

Atmospherepress.com

Preface

by Colman McCarthy

In more than thirty-five years of teaching Peace Studies cours-
es in Washington, DC, area high schools and universities, I've
had the bracing fortune of hosting well over a hundred guest
speakers in my classes. They have ranged from Nobel Peace
Prize winners and major league baseball players to women
and men who care for the broke and broken in the nation's
homeless shelters. Come tell us your stories, I ask the guests.
Few have related to my students as well, as emotionally and as
instantly as Eddie Ellis.

It wasn't long after his release, after fifteen years of being
caged in prisons that included supermaxes in Colorado and
Virginia, that Eddie became a regular visitor nearly every se-
mester beginning in 2008 in my classes at Bethesda-Chevy
Chase High, Wilson High School, American University, the
University of Maryland and Georgetown Law and my inter-
national classes. As Eddie speaks, little time is needed for my
students to realize that it isn't what we achieve in life that
matters; it's what we overcome.

Students wonder why Eddie is moving forward and not
recidivating because of a parole violation or another crime,
as is all but routine for large numbers of the released. For
Eddie, it appears to be a combination of help from within and
without. While in prison, he became a reader, one who found
satisfaction in opening his mind to ideas that energized him to
make further explorations of the spirit. He had a mother who

never gave up on him, whether it was after he seemed lost at age sixteen in a juvenile prison or stashed in an isolation cell. On leaving prison, he found probation officers who were both professionally skilled and personally caring. He speaks also of having a higher power in his life, "One who has allowed me to make it through my situation. When you return to the world after fifteen years, you are really playing catch-up. I had to learn how to ride the Metro, go on job interviews. It's still hard to be around a lot of people. Trusting anyone is difficult. If I go to a restaurant, I need to sit with my back to the wall. I had to learn to deal with my family. In a lot of ways, I'm still learning how to be free."

To show their gratitude to Eddie, I ask my students to write letters of appreciation to him—handwritten letters, not emailed, not texted, not smartphone.

A fourth-year student from American University wrote: "Dear Mr. Ellis: I want to tell you that I was struck by your humility and honesty in describing your difficult experience. Retelling these stories may not be easy for you, but you are doing our society a service by showing that our paths are winding and not linear, and that people can mend their lives for the better. You are an inspiration to me and to countless others who may find themselves adrift from their roots and values."

Eddie's successful work to help the formerly incarcerated heal the scars and traumas of imprisonment through his non-profit One by 1, moved a Georgetown Law student to write: "I really enjoyed hearing about your perspective on the criminal justice system and your efforts to improve the re-entry prospects for the newly released individuals. This past summer I worked with the American Civil Liberties Union on criminal justice reform. Many of the things we did focus on pushing for legislation that would improve the various re-entry programs around the country, with the goal of reducing recidivism rates by acknowledging the struggles that most people face straight out of prison with little or no training for the modern workforce. It is encouraging to know that advocates like you are fighting for the same goals I had at the ACLU. I truly believe your efforts will make a great deal of difference to many."

In all his visits to my classes, Eddie never came off as preachy, much less as a know-it-all. Instead, he displayed an engaging manner and an endearing sense of humor. Many times, he came with his wife Camille, who was equally endearing. This from another law student: "Maybe I'm wrong, but I doubt many in your shoes would be able to share what you have been through, and for that I admire you. I think you are brave. When I think of you, I cannot help but recall my two brothers, who were not that much older than you when they were at Westland Middle School. They were lucky to have stayed out of trouble, but I see little difference between you and them really. Please keep on your path. It is true, honest and good. You have my love and support along the way, always." What follows in these pages is both a soulful story and an enduring piece of literature.

Introduction

My name is Eddie B. Ellis Jr. and I am a forty-seven-year-old Black man. I am the father of three beautiful children and married to a fabulous woman by the name of Camille. I am very grateful for every day I have on the outside of those prison walls after fifteen years in that dehumanizing place.

In 2005, I started working on my book while I was in the ADX Supermax prison in Florence, Colorado, while trying to maintain my sanity because this prison was built to be destructive; mentally, physically and emotionally. Writing was one of my many outlets while in prison, and it became an escape mechanism that allowed me to go wherever I wanted to go.

I ran into a lot of roadblocks while working on my book. One day, the correctional officers were conducting a shakedown and this day they selected my cell to search. They handcuffed me, took me out of the cell, and told me to face the wall. I could hear the officers in my cell talking, and I was listening as much as I could to what they were saying with all the other inmates talking and yelling out of their cell doors. I was not really concerned because I didn't have anything in there to worry about, but out of nowhere one of the officers said, "Ellis, I knocked over a cup of water that was on your desk and it spilled on some papers."

When they removed the handcuffs, I went over to clean up the water and saw that the pages of my book had been destroyed.

It took me nearly ten months to start to work on my book

again, but then I lost my Uncle Toney. It took the wind out of me for a few months. At the same time, my parole was revoked. Still, I dug down and allowed that pen to make music with that paper. And I kept writing.

At times I still wonder how I went from being sentenced to twenty-two years in prison, to being locked down in solitary confinement twenty-three hours a day for over ten years, to finishing this book. And then becoming a motivational speaker, an advocate for those returning home from prison, and a married man with an unwavering love for my kids.

Today I am in Washington DC, in Hains Point Park, enjoying being out and about, enjoying being free! As I walk around this park and observe all that's going on, all the people enjoying being outside and in nature, I have a better appreciation for life. I must admit, it's an amazing feeling to be able to see mothers push their babies in strollers, kids flying kites, and cyclists riding their bikes. This is something I was deprived of for many years. Hains Point Park, a place I've known since I was a child, sits on the East Potomac River in Washington, DC. The scenery brings me peace. The sound of the water relaxes me in ways unimaginable, while the thought of catching a fish fuel my competitive nature.

Often, when I come out here, I do a lot of reflecting on my life. The good and the bad. The ups and downs. The trials and tribulations. I wonder about my father who was killed when I was just a baby. I think about my beautiful mother who made so many sacrifices for me over the years. I look up to the sky and thank God for my loving wife, Camille, my little man, Eddie III and my two step-kids, who have brought me so much happiness. But, most of all, I think about the changes that I've made in my life and how I can continue to make a difference in the lives of others.

I wrote this memoir because I want to tell my story, especially because it shows that it is truly possible for change to happen, even for someone who has been sent away to prison for a long time. Despite being in prison, I have changed because I worked at it and accepted the support of others inside and outside the prisons and the inspiration of a higher power.

I hope this story inspires others to survive and thrive beyond prison.

PART
one

Childhood

I was born on Stanton Road in Southeast DC in July 1975 to my parents, Eddie Sr. and Sheila. They were very young when they met and, by the time I was born, they were both only twenty years old. I was the first grandchild on my mother's side of the family and the only grandson on my father's side, and, as a result, I was indeed spoiled and a shared baby. Everyone wanted to spend time with me. My aunts, grandparents, and all of my mother's friends wanted me at their house.

Naturally, I spent the most time with my mother and grandparents. In my early days, I lived with my grandmother on my mom's side, Annette, and my grandfather, Clarence Sr. Grandma Annette had ten kids and she was truly the matriarch of the family. She was an educated woman and, along with my grandfather, gave my mom the support she needed. My grandmother was short in stature but had a voice and spirit that could stop a truck in its tracks. She loved her family and would do anything to make things better for us. My grandfather was a slim, short man who did his best to support his family even though he fell short at times until his death in the mid-80s.

Despite the support my grandparents offered, I still had challenges as a baby. When I was very young, sudden infant death syndrome (SIDS) almost took my life on several occasions. The first time, I was strapped in my car seat, riding with my mother and grandmother. My mother turned to look at me, and that's when she noticed that my face was the same color as the blue snow suit I had on and that I wasn't breathing. She gave me CPR and tried her best to resuscitate me, but to no avail. My mother told me that she was frantic and didn't know what to do.

The paramedics arrived, gave me oxygen, and then took me to DC General Hospital. The doctors ran tests, said I was fine and released me the same day. But, as soon as my mother got me home, the same thing happened. I was blue in the face and not breathing. The paramedics came again, and that time I was rushed to the Children's Hospital, the place where I ultimately spent the following eight months hooked up to machines.

At the time, sudden infant death syndrome was fairly new to doctors, and they really didn't know what to do to treat it. In fact, my mother told me that I was one of the first babies in DC to be hooked up to a machine that monitored my breathing around the clock. Every time I stopped breathing the machine alerted the doctors and gave me the oxygen I needed. My mom stayed by my side for most of those eight months; she was given a bed in the hospital so she could be near me. The doctors were never able to figure out what caused my illness, but I didn't have another near-death experience once I was released.

It was only a few months after I was discharged from the hospital that my family and I experienced a horrible loss. My father was murdered. I was two years old at the time of my father's death – too young to remember anything about him, but I've been told that he was a cool guy and that we have some of the same characteristics. Unfortunately, he fell victim to the gun violence that has left many kids fatherless in inner cities across America. Despite my father's death, his mother, Ella Mae and my grandfather Moe were very supportive and helped my mother when they could. My grandfather, Moe Ellis, was a quiet, slender man who was very strong and athletic for his age. He worked hard, took care of their home and especially enjoyed spending time with his grandchildren and taking us to North Carolina to meet his side of the family. My grandmother Ella Mae was a confident woman who loved to dress.

She enjoyed taking her grandchildren out to eat and also loved taking holiday photos together.

I forged a strong bond with my grandparents even though my dad wasn't around, and I'm sure I learned a lot about resilience from my grandmother, Ella Mae. She was taken out of school by her parents at an early age because they needed help on the farm down in North Carolina. However, she didn't let that stop her from progressing and earning a living as an adult. She learned to do hair and eventually owned a nice salon on 14th Street in Northwest DC. My grandfather was a working man as well. He worked for Colonial Parking for over fifty years and loved his job. He worked his way up from parking cars to becoming a supervisor in his time there.

I attended several elementary schools when I was growing up because we moved a few times as my mom was figuring things out as a young mother. The first school I attended was a daycare inside Eastern High School in Northeast DC. At the time, my Aunt Aretha, her husband Jim, and my Aunt Frances were all students at the school. Jim played football and ran track. Aretha ran track as well, so I would often go and watch them compete. They'd also come down and check on me during their lunch and sometimes took me home after school.

It was around 1980 that I left the daycare and went on to Minor Elementary School. Once again, I had a good support system while I was there because my grandmother Annette worked at the school and was the supervisor of the crossing guards. She would drive my uncle and me to school, but once we got comfortable, we walked ourselves. At the time I loved school and enjoyed running around playing with my friends. But I also remember getting into two fights on the playground. I don't know why, but getting into it with others is something that I couldn't dodge, even as a kid.

One thing I recall the most about that school is one day I went into my grandmother's classroom and stole one of the crossing guard's belts. For two days I stood on the corner and helped kids cross the street and had the time of my life. It made me feel important. Back then it was a big deal for a kid to get a crossing guard job, and I relished the opportunity. In DC, there weren't many school buses, and most kids walked home from school. Unfortunately, it didn't take long for my grandmother to find out about my new profession, and it wasn't pretty. She disciplined me and gave me a good tongue-lashing.

"What were you thinking, Eddie?" she exclaimed. "Those crossing guards are trained and taught how to help people get across the street in a safe way. You haven't had that kind of training; you could have gotten someone hurt or worse! Please don't do that again."

As a nine year old, all I could do was cry and apologize to my grandmother because I was wrong and had let her down. I felt so bad. I looked up at her with tears in my eyes, and she grabbed me and gave me a big hug and said, "Baby, I love you. Now head on home!" It wasn't too bad of an experience, but let's just say I learned my lesson about being sneaky around Grandma Annette.

I started going to Wheatley in the third or fourth grade, and I remember that I got into a fight the first week I was there. I was out on the playground with a bunch of kids, and one of them tried to bully me. This tall kid came up close and shoved me hard.

I stepped back and looked hard at him. "Why did you push me?" I said.

He shrugged and said, "I'll do it again. Watch me."

Within those seconds, everything my uncles told me about protecting myself came into my mind, and I jumped on him and beat him up until the teachers pulled me off. I had beaten him up really good, and he never bothered me again. I remember being happy that I stood up for myself, but I hated the way I felt in that moment. I got a kick out of beating him up, and the anger that I felt started to become normal to me.

I had a lot of friends who went to Wheatley because we

all played together at the Number 9 Boys and Girls Club and outside in the neighborhood. It was there that I met one of my favorite teachers, Ms. Washington. Ms. Washington was a short black woman who had a voice of thunder. It was clear that she took teaching very seriously and that she cared about us. She made us feel safe around her. She fed students that needed to eat. She did hair for some students that needed their hair done. Ms. Washington was so special to me because I could see that she was trying to build up these little black children that she was teaching.

One day she asked the class who wanted to go horseback riding, and I raised my hand. Even as a kid, I had a love for animals. Shortly thereafter, she arranged for us to get into a horseback riding class at Rock Creek Park, which is the oldest natural urban park in the National Park System and a staple in DC. Eight kids from my class joined the class at the stable to learn how to ride a horse. None of us had ever ridden a horse before in our lives. When we walked into the stable and saw those huge horses tied to the gate with saddles on their backs, we were all terrified and ready to get right back onto the bus that brought us to the horse stable.

Before we could head back to the bus, a tall white lady walked up to where we were standing and said, "Have any of you ever ridden a horse before?"

"No!!" we all said.

She told us to grab an apple out of this old box that was beside the gate, and we did.

"Now, everyone, hold your hand like mine – palm up and your fingers pointing down and allow the apple to sit on your hand. Pretty soon the horse will take it out of your hand."

After what seemed like two hours, we all allowed the horses to take the apples out of our hands.

That helped us get over being scared. So, after that, we got on the horses and rode around in a dirt ring for thirty minutes. We took those classes for three weeks and had so much fun. The big animals that we feared so much made all of us feel so safe. I had a great time learning something new, and over the years I've maintained my love for horses.

It was also around that time that I really started to think about my father's death even more. I was two years old when my father was shot and killed. Because I was so young when it happened, my mother wanted to protect me and had never told me the circumstances surrounding his passing.

However, one day when I was eight years old, I was playing with one of my cousins, and she got mad and said, "That's why your daddy is dead. He got killed." I couldn't believe what I'd heard. Those words stung.

Of course, my cousin and I got over our little spat, but sometimes I don't know if I ever really recovered from that revelation. After that, I became angry. I wanted to hurt the person that killed my father. I spoke with my mother about the incident, and she became upset. She said that she was going to tell me when she felt I was old enough to handle the pain of his death. She told me how much she missed him and how she wished he was still alive. And then, out of nowhere, a tear rolled down her face. I hated to see her cry. I'll never forget talking to her about it that day. Since then, I haven't talked to my mom about his passing because I always think about the pain that was on her face that day.

I stayed at Wheatley for two years, and then we moved to Minnesota Avenue in the southeast section of the city. Going to Kimball was rough on me because I left all my friends and teachers. Southeast was known to be the craziest part of the city, and I didn't get along with the kids there like I did in my old neighborhood. The first day that I came outside, all the kids were checking me out, looking me up and down. I went to the basketball court and started playing with some kids; but soon I noticed that one of them was being a bit rough with me. Instead of playing fair, he was fouling, pushing, and just trying to take the ball. We fought on that day and probably on ten occasions after that.

While I was at Kimball Elementary, I was tested, and the results showed that I had dyslexia. I didn't know what that was. I also was dealing with depression then because I always thought about my dad. I found myself losing interest in school because I wasn't getting the help that I needed. School wasn't fun because I wasn't learning at the same pace as my friends. When I was younger, I used to see words backwards, numbers were mixed up, and I just saw things differently than others around me. Noticing those things made me feel different and very insecure, and I didn't like that at all.

Finally, in a meeting at the school, my mother and I were told by the teacher that I had to be placed in special education classes. All I knew about special education was that the kids acted crazy, fought all the time, and the classrooms were loud. I didn't want to be in there because everyone thought the kids were strange. I didn't want people to look at me that way. I cried and fussed because I wanted to be in regular classes and just like all the other kids.

Academically, I felt lost, even if my teacher told me that I did a good job. I know that had a huge effect on my self-esteem, but I did a lot to cover up my shortcomings. I often acted out to try to divert attention from my learning problems. I refused to participate, put my head down, or passed the time talking. I got help for my disability, but I don't think it did much. My mom came to the school to make sure I was getting the help I needed, but there was only so much that she could do, and the teachers were already overwhelmed. She also spent time reading with me and helping me at home. I know it was hard for her because she couldn't explain why those things were happening to me. I was very eager to learn and just wanted to be like all the other kids. Over time I lost hope and confidence.

Other than that, my childhood was like the lives of other kids in my Washington, DC, neighborhood. I enjoyed playing football, going to Number 9 Boys and Girls Club, playing tag, and walking to the store with my friends. My mom, along with the help of my grandmothers and other family members, did their best to provide for me and give me all the support I needed. However, I always felt the void of not having my father in my life. I really can't explain that feeling, but it's a place of emptiness.

As a child I used to love camping, fishing and just being around my family. Like most kids, I loved to be outside playing sports and hanging out with my friends. Mark was one of my best friends back then, and he loved sports as well. One weekend when I was about eleven years old, I was supposed to spend the night over at his house. I couldn't wait until I got home from school. I was so happy I couldn't focus on my work like I needed to. All that I could think about was the fun that we were going to have. Once three o'clock came, I ran out of the school and down the street to my house. Once in, I put my books away and immediately gathered my overnight clothes. But, to my surprise, my mom changed her mind and didn't let me go. She told me that I had to spend the night another time. I was so mad. I had been looking forward to that day the entire week.

On that night I was very upset with my mom, and it showed in my actions. I was a bit disrespectful and had an attitude. I went to sleep mad and woke up very early the next morning so that I could go outside and hook up with Mark. When I opened the front door, my dog ran past me out the door. I called for "Pup" to come back, but he went around the corner to Mark's house, and I followed. Unfortunately, when I got to the corner, I saw a lot of police and medical vehicles at his home. I didn't know what was going on. His mother was crying and walking down the steps from their house to where the police and medical people were.

A very haunted feeling came upon me. I'd never felt anything like that before. I looked back at the house, and I saw two medical people holding a gurney with a body under a bloody sheet. I really started to get worried because I still hadn't seen Mark. His mother called my name, and I walked over to her. She reached her arms out to me and told me Mark was in a better place. I looked at her very confused because, at eleven years old, I didn't understand what she was saying to me. I started to cry. I asked her where Mark was, and she told me that they were putting him in the van and that someone had shot and killed him. At that point I became even more upset. I later found out that some guys stormed into the house and killed him because of something his father had done. I was shocked and scared by this.

But that wasn't my only experience with violent deaths as a kid.

The following summer, a lot of people in my neighborhood were just out enjoying a nice day. Everyone was just hanging out and having a good time. Suddenly, I heard loud voices and looked down the street. There was a confrontation going on. Everyone walked over to the commotion, and as I got closer, I heard a loud bang. It was a gunshot. I immediately froze and watched my friend's grandmother fall to the ground. I heard people yelling and saw others running, but I couldn't move. I started to cry, and then my Aunt Marsha pulled my arm. It seemed like her snatching me was what woke me up. That experience really bothered me because Ms. Smith was a good woman. She took care of her family, went to church, and also showed love to the kids in the community. I will always have a place in my heart for that nice lady.

Trouble

As soon as I turned fourteen, my life began to take a turn for the worse. It was around this age that I began feeling an immense amount of anger. My demeanor became aggressive. My mother told me that I used to cry a lot and that I always talked about wanting to find who killed my dad. Not to mention, I was stubborn and had a chip on my shoulder. I was going through a lot mentally that I didn't understand.

On top of all that, I began to surround myself with the wrong crowd. I hung around the street guys in the neighborhood. Drug dealers, robbers, and individuals who'd rather commit crimes than go to school. Along with my uncles on my mother's side, these were the type of guys I started to look up to then. In the past, I had always looked up to one particular uncle because when we were younger we did a lot of things together – fishing, riding bikes in the neighborhood and just hanging out. That had meant a lot to me. But this same uncle had fallen short by becoming a part of the streets like those other guys who had the pretty girls, nice cars, and lived a lifestyle that was intriguing to my young eyes. Now the streets started to become a reality of mine.

Everyone encouraged me to stay out of the streets, but I was bull-headed and wouldn't listen. Looking back on things, I believe my father was the only one I probably would've listened to. However, he was gone and that made me vulnerable. My mother tried and did her best to figure out what was going on with me. She even took me to a therapist to seek counseling, but that didn't work. As a child I didn't think it was cool to talk about my problems. I felt as though others would see that as a sign of weakness. In my mind, I believed that boys were supposed to be strong and tough, while whining was for girls. The problem with that was I didn't know what to do with all of those built-up emotions. Many times, they bubbled up and came out in an angry or aggressive manner.

At home, the relationship between my mother and me deteriorated fast. She worked a lot and loved me the way a mother should; yet I was getting into more and more trouble. I came home late, got bad grades, and fought a lot. Most of the conflicts I had stemmed from anger. Other kids thought I was a pretty boy and couldn't fight, so that forced me to prove to others that I could stand up for myself. In my neighborhood, being tough is how you earned your respect, and I wasn't going to let anyone get out on me.

As time went on, my mother decided that it was time to move away from the city. It was getting too dangerous. We moved to Silver Spring, MD. Her goal was to provide a better life for us. Silver Spring, located in Montgomery County, is one of the most affluent counties in the country. Moving there was a tough transition for me because it was the total opposite of living in the city. Although it's located just minutes from DC, Maryland is a totally different world. The first revelation was that there were more white people than blacks. DC had always been known as Chocolate City, and blacks outnumbered whites by the thousands.

I had grown accustomed to being around people who looked, talked, and dressed like me. But most of the black kids in Maryland were raised differently. Many of them grew up in nice neighborhoods and hadn't experienced a lot of the things I'd gone through. They hadn't been exposed to drugs, guns, and all that comes with living in the city. They didn't need to stand on the corner and sell drugs to make money for their families. Their parents had nice jobs and could afford to buy them what they wanted. I felt like an outcast. I was uncomfortable about who I was as a young black male. My identity was lost. I didn't know if I was Eddie, the kid from DC, or Eddie, the kid who didn't fit in with his new group of peers.

At school I felt like more of an outcast than I did in the special education classes. Not only did I have to deal with being ostracized by my peers, I also felt that way with my teachers and the administrators. But, on the first day of school I met a guy named Leon at the bus stop. We introduced ourselves, joked around, and just talked about regular stuff. I began to think that going to Westland Middle School might not be as bad as I thought it would. Then, I went into the office to get the schedule for my classes. A black administrator handed me my schedule and immediately said, "Eddie, please don't bring that DC stuff out here." My enthusiasm was immediately gone. I hadn't even done anything, and I already felt like I had a target on my back. It would've been nice if she'd said, "Welcome to Westland, Eddie. I look forward to working with you and helping you have a productive year."

It was then that I knew I was in for an uphill battle. Those suburban people really didn't understand me, and I honestly didn't understand them. It's sad to say, but we weren't a good match. I was a black kid from the city, and they were uppity suburban soccer moms. We clashed, and it was a recipe for disaster. My mother fought so hard for me at that school, and I felt bad. She was always there to support me when I had incidents with teachers. She believed that the white teachers just didn't understand how to communicate with me. They weren't accustomed to a kid with my personality, and the fact that I was dyslexic and not interested in school made matters worse.

Things weren't all bad though. I played basketball for the team at Westland, and it was a lot of fun. I remember one day on the basketball court at lunchtime, a dude that most people at the school feared started talking trash to me. I didn't back down and let him know we could get it on whenever he was ready. He walked away talking shit, probably surprised that I responded in the manner that I did. Later in the day I saw him in the gym, and the dude was still talking shit. The gym teacher was a kick boxer, and she had boxing gloves laying around. The fake bully asked me if I wanted to put them on, and I did. I beat his ass with those gloves on. He was very strong but had no boxing skills. I countered every punch that he threw.

After it was over, he walked off mad and said something slick. I just laughed at him and the followers that he surrounded himself with. Later I found out that he told people he would beat my ass without the gloves the next time we saw one another. The tension started to rise between this dude, the school bully, his flunkies and me. My buddies Leon and Chris were thrown into the mix as well because we all hung together.

Weeks went on, and the bully and flunkies kept on talking crap; one day I was told that one of them had a knife in their locker and planned to stab me. I wasn't scared. On that day I told the bully and all his friends to go to a field after school so we could fight. None of them came. So, for the next week I went after all of them at different times one by one to show them that I wasn't playing. I ended up fighting two of those guys and slapped up a Spanish kid who hung out with them. I learned at an early age that sometimes you have to take your respect.

After that incident, Leon and I became even closer. One day he and I were in a girl's building waiting for her and her friend to come out because we were all going to the mall. Out of nowhere, a man came out of his apartment being disrespectful to us for no reason. I was trying to stay cool when he walked up in my face, but I couldn't. He was too close to me, and I couldn't wait to see what he was going to do. I cocked back and punched him, slitting his eye. I saw him grab his side, which made me think that he was going for a gun. I jumped on him and beat him some more. Then I walked away. I went to the community recreation center to chill out and let things calm down.

Shortly thereafter, one of my friends came to get me because the police were trying to kick in my apartment door. I went home to face what was going on, and when I got close by, I saw about five police cars. I walked up and asked, "Are you looking for me?"

An officer said, "Who are you?"

"Eddie Ellis," I replied.

The officer told me to put my hands up, and I did. As I did that, I saw the dude I beat up start to walk towards me. I kicked my leg out, and he fell. Then the officer threw me in the car. I was locked up and charged with assault. The case was later dropped because everyone that was there told the police that the guy came to us in a very threatening way, and I acted in self-defense.

A few weeks went by and everything was going smoothly, until one day when I was in gym class and chose to sit out. I didn't have my gym clothes, and I wasn't going to do a bunch of running in regular clothes. My teacher, a white lady, said, "Buckwheat, you are going to do what I tell you to do." I snapped. I pushed her away from me, and the police were called. I was taken out of school in handcuffs.

It was also around that time that my uncle was shot. An old friend called me and told me what had taken place. My uncle was standing outside talking to some people when a car stopped near him, and someone got out and started shooting. My uncle was hit, though he probably wasn't the target.

By that time, at the age of fifteen, I was giving up on life, and I headed to the streets to seek revenge. This was the start of my downfall!

My uncle got shot in the head, but luckily, he survived. He was one of the family members I looked up to the most, and when I went to my grandmother's house, I spent a lot of time with him. Although he was a few years older than I was, we seemed to have a lot in common. He was a man of principle who was respected, and I loved that about him. The moment I heard he got shot; my life changed. I had blood in my eyes. I wanted revenge. I wanted to return the favor and put a bullet in the person who'd shot him. At the time, my friends and I were getting into all sorts of trouble. We were involved in dealing drugs, smoking weed, drinking, and so many other risky things. I was out of control. The crime rate in DC was at an all-time high, and the district was known as the murder capital.

The crack epidemic penetrated the streets just as in all other inner-city neighborhoods across America. The drugs created a surge of violence in record amounts as killings, shootings, and overall crime soared. Rival crews shot and killed one another over territory. Everyday working people who'd never committed a crime in their life smoked crack, lost their jobs, and became zombies. Even the beloved Mayor of DC, Marion Berry, was videotaped smoking crack cocaine and was arrested by the FBI. Many residents had respect and love for him. He cared about the community wholeheartedly, but that just goes to show how prevalent crime and drugs in the city were.

No surprise that soon my delinquent ways caught up with me, and I ended up in a juvenile detention center. I was arrested for armed robbery, a crime I didn't commit. My friends and I caught a taxi and were going to the movies in Georgetown, an upscale section of the city. We were in the back of the car, just laughing and joking. Suddenly we came upon a police roadblock. For no reason the cab driver just went crazy. He started screaming and jumped out of the cab running towards the police. The police charged over to the car with their guns drawn and ordered us out of the car. They ordered us to get on the ground. While I was on the ground, the Alcohol, Tobacco and Firearms officer put his foot on my back and told me not to move or else. The ground was scorching hot, and my hands burned. The cab driver told the police that we were going to rob him. I couldn't believe it. We had no intention of robbing that man.

I was taken to Seton Hall Youth Detention Center and charged with armed robbery. I stayed at that facility for a few months, and then I was taken to the notorious Oak Hill Youth Detention Center. The facility was a place where all the young robbers, killers, and delinquents went. Anyone who knows about Oak Hill will tell you that it is a dangerous place. I knew I would have to fight and defend myself as soon as I arrived. Sadly, that's just the way things are when you're locked up.

In Oak Hill, there were two things that I knew were certain. I knew I was going to see someone that I had beef with, and I knew that someone would try to jump out there and do some dumb mess. I was right. I got into several fights during the few months I was there. To be honest, that place made me even more violent. Luckily, the charges against me were eventually dropped, and I was released on August 23rd, 1991. By the time I came home I didn't fear anything, and I was angry at a system that had wrongly accused me of a crime that I hadn't committed.

After my release, I attended Woodland Job Corps, which was right down the street from Oak Hill. I met Kevin on my first day in Job Corps, and he was a cool guy. We kicked it in there, and over the years we remained friends. But I knew that I wouldn't be there for long. At Job Corps, I acted like I was still at Oak Hill and was eventually kicked out for fighting a staff member and other students. I really didn't care because I wanted to get back on the streets and get my hands dirty. By that time, running the streets had become a way of life for me. I thought it was the cool thing to do. I was only sixteen, and my mind hadn't fully matured enough to see how self-destructive my lifestyle had become to myself, my family and my community. During these years when my brain was so immature and my thinking so fueled by anger, I just didn't fully comprehend the impact and consequences of my actions as I do now as a forty-seven-year-old.

Not long after my release, I ran away from home and lived with my grandmother off and on. At the time she lived on 13th and Irving Street Northwest. I stayed with her and my friends from the neighborhood. My mother tried to get me to come back home on several occasions. She'd come looking for me, but I always managed to slither away before she got her hands on me. I thought that I was doing what was best for me at the time. I didn't want to bring the negativity I was involved in home to my mother and brother.

Several months later, on December 20, 1991, I did something that forever changed the course of my life. A friend of mine borrowed a gun from a guy in the neighborhood. I will not use the name of the deceased out of respect for his family. My friend refused to give the gun back to the guy, and that's how the whole mess started.

One day my friend fired the gun, then took off running and hid it. The police heard the shots, came and questioned us, and then went on about their business because we told them that we didn't have a gun. Later the owner of the gun came to retrieve his weapon, but my friend told him the police took it. The guy became angry and threatened him. He told him he'd better give him his gun back or else.

I got caught up in the middle of it because this guy was my friend, and because of that, the owner of the gun threatened me as well. I told him I didn't have anything to do with the issue and that he gave the gun to my buddy, not me. But he insisted that I was just as guilty as my friend and that **WE** stole his gun. I had to stand with my friend because that's what friends do, but at the same time I had to let the guy know that my friend and I were two separate people.

Over the course of a couple of weeks, this guy threatened my life and told me I'd better get his gun back. Every time he did, I told him that I had nothing to do with him giving the gun to my friend and to leave me out of it. He didn't believe me, and subsequently, I became a target for no reason. I knew he was serious when one afternoon, I was walking down the street, and he was the passenger in a vehicle that slowly rolled up on the side of me. He lowered the window, hollered profanities, and pointed a Mac-10 machine gun in my direction. He didn't fire the weapon, but he was sending me a message. After that, I knew there was a serious problem, so I bought a gun to protect myself. I didn't know what this guy planned to do. Days went by without me seeing him.

But all of that changed when I went with the same friend to a party in the Adams Morgan section of the city. By the time I arrived at the apartment where the party was supposed to be that night, the party had been canceled. My friend and I were leaving the building when we spotted the guy who'd threatened my life days earlier. He was with two of his friends. In an effort to squash the beef, my buddy tried to give him a gun to replace the one that he'd taken, but he didn't want it. Once again, he made threats and demanded his weapon. Suddenly, he reached into his waistband and pulled out a gun. Fearing that my life was in danger, I pulled out my gun, fired several shots and watched him fall to the ground along with one of his friends. I was in such a state of shock that it wasn't until I was two blocks away that I realized I still had the gun in my hand.

After the shooting, I ran to my girlfriend's house and immediately started smoking marijuana to try to clear my mind and think of my next move. I was frantic and needed to calm down. She could sense something was wrong and wanted to know what had happened, but I wouldn't tell her. I didn't know what to say. I was completely numb. I'd just shot someone.

A few hours later, I was sitting on the couch watching TV when there was a knock on the door, and my stomach dropped. My heart was already racing, but it quickly hit full throttle. I paced the room, not knowing what to do. It was the guy's friends who I had just shot, and they were angry. They told my girl that I had killed their friend. Up to that point, all I knew was that I had shot him. I didn't know that he was dead until they said so. After I heard that he had passed, I honestly didn't know what to feel. My girl told me that she was going to call the police, but I begged her not to. I knew there were witnesses, and if the police came, I would surely be identified as the shooter.

Soon thereafter, there was another knock at the door. It was law enforcement. My girl let them in, and they began to question her. She told them that a group of guys had come to her door. The cops left, and I threw the gun I shot the guy with out of the apartment window. I figured that if they didn't catch me with the weapon, then they wouldn't be able to charge me with the crime.

Little did I know they could still charge someone with a crime without a weapon. They never found the gun. A short time later, the police showed back up at the door, and this time homicide detectives were with them. They forced their way into the apartment, asked me a few questions, handcuffed me, and went into the backroom to see who else was there. They brought my friend out in handcuffs and put us in the backseat of a squad car.

As I sat there, the last hour of my life replayed in my head. The argument in front of the apartment building. The shooting. The guy fell to the ground. The blood coming out of the side of his neck. I didn't know what was going to happen next.

At the homicide unit, the detectives really pressured me to confess. They used all the crafty tactics that are used in interrogation rooms. They tried the good cop, bad cop role. They cursed, threatened, and tried to get me to talk for hours. Finally, one of the detectives got angry and stormed out of the room. The other one followed. Upon returning, they told me the game was over. They read me my rights. At sixteen years old, I was charged as an adult with the crime of murder in the first degree.

DC Jail, North 1 Juvenile Block, Cell 44, top right, was my new temporary home.

Behind Bars

I'd heard many stories about DC Jail, but they didn't do any justice to what I witnessed. The jail was filthy, cockroach-infested and smelled disgusting. It's an old jail, so it was just run down. It was wintertime when I arrived, so the facility was very cold. The first thing I noticed was that the inmates were out of control. I quickly realized that I was in an unsafe environment and that I could be harmed at any moment. I had a lot of old beef, but after the murder, I knew I probably had new enemies as well. Before my friend had the incident with the victim, I'd never communicated with him. He wasn't an associate of mine. I knew that he probably had friends and family members who were locked up and that they may have known who I was. Therefore, I had to man-up and mentally prepare myself for whatever was to come.

In the DC Jail, everyone wanted to be tough and earn a reputation. I knew that. I had the mentality that I was going to do any and everything to protect myself. While there, I got into several fights. I won some, and I lost some, but not protecting myself was never an option. I made a knife out of a broken piece of metal on my second day there. I sharpened it throughout the night. I knew there was a good possibility that I'd have to stab someone. That's just the way my mentality was at the time. I would rather have gotten caught with a knife by the correction officers than gotten caught without it by someone who wanted to take my life.

My first few days there were rough. I couldn't sleep, and I had nightmares of the shooting. Although I did it out of self-defense, I was sixteen years old and had to live with the fact that I'd taken someone's life. I was remorseful. At times I felt like I was losing my mind. I couldn't grasp the concept of what I'd done. Everything just happened so fast. My goal was to go to a party and have a good time. Instead, I ended up killing someone and going to jail. I thought about all those things, but I had to be strong. I had the upcoming trial on my mind.

My mother made many sacrifices when she paid for my lawyer. She wanted to ensure that I got a fair trial. I remember the first visit that I had with her while I was in jail. It was stressful. The phone was tapped, and I could only talk with her behind the glass barrier.

"What is going on, Eddie?" she asked. "What happened?" I could see the pain and hurt on her face.

"Ma, I was put in a situation where I had to defend myself. I'm sorry." We both broke down and began to cry. In that moment, I wasn't a tough guy. I reverted to Eddie, the sixteen-year-old kid who wanted to reach out and give my mother a hug. I wanted her to be able to tell me that everything would be okay, like she did when I was younger. But she couldn't utter those words to me. We both knew that everything wasn't going to be okay.

"Eddie, you know I didn't raise you to do no mess like that. Someone has lost their life, and somebody's mother, father and entire family is out there hurting. This ain't right, baby. You're my son, and I love you, but you have taken someone's life."

I didn't know what to say. I just cried. The tears poured from both of our eyes. "I love you, Ma," were the only words that I could muster up.

It still hurts me today to think about the pain I put her through. My mother has always been a hardworking woman for as long as I've known her. We had our differences, but I was a mama's boy, and I have no shame in saying that. She was always there for me, through thick and thin. But there wasn't anything she could've done to get me out of the situation that I'd put myself in. I put my family in a tough position.

It also broke my heart to think that I wouldn't be able to be there for my little brother. Before I went to jail, we were close. I took him everywhere and was his protector. It really hurt me to think of being away from him during the time I'd be gone. But I knew I was in trouble. I couldn't believe that at sixteen years old, I was facing seventy-five years to life if convicted of first-degree murder.

My trial started in March 1992. The lawyers for myself and my friend, who was now my codefendant, planned to argue that this was a case of self-defense. There was evidence that the person who lost his life was in possession of a gun and pulled out his weapon on us. We were both offered fifteen-year plea bargains before the trial started, but we were confident that we could beat the charges. I knew my self-defense claim was strong, but I still didn't know how my day in court would turn out. Juries can be tricky, and prosecutors can be crafty at manipulating facts.

At six a.m., on a cold Tuesday morning, a correctional officer came to my cell and told me I had to get ready so I could arrive at the DC Superior courthouse by seven a.m., even though I was scheduled to be in court at nine a.m. I rolled out of my bed, looked out the window at the dark sky, and said a short prayer before I started to brush my teeth and wash my face.

After I got dressed, I went to the TV room, ate breakfast, and watched a little bit of the news. At the time I smoked cigarettes, so after I was done, I went back to my cell to grab my Newports. I lit my cigarette and headed down to my friend Cut's cell. When I got to his cell, I kicked the bars and startled him. We started laughing, but the situation quickly turned serious as he knew I was on my way to court. We talked about my trial, and he asked me how I felt. I told him I was worried and stressed. He told me to pray and that everything would be okay. I let him know that I had mixed feelings. I hoped for the best but was prepared for the worst. Cut was locked up for murder as well and was due to begin his trial weeks later, so he understood just how nervous I was feeling.

My intention was to go to his cell, smoke a cigarette and head out to court. But we ended up smoking four or five cigarettes while waiting for me to be picked up. Finally, the CO called my name and told me it was time to leave. Before I left, I went to the cells of all the people I was close to and told them to wish me luck.

On that day, there were three other juveniles going to court, and I paid close attention to who they were. I always had to be aware of my surroundings there because top left and top right in the Juvenile Block were always going to war with each other, even though many of us had friends and foes on both sides. If you were caught slipping, you could get beaten down or stabbed. It was very easy to get sucker punched or stabbed when small groups gathered. But that's just how things were because a lot of people in the jail didn't get along.

Luckily, I had no issues with the other guys. I also saw my codefendant, Tim, and at first we just looked at each other. Then I hugged him and said that we were going to be okay, even though I really wasn't at all sure we would come out of this okay or not as far as the court went.

We went into an area called the sally port and waited for a correctional officer to come to get us. Before he even appeared, I could hear his keys rattling. Finally, there he was, calling us out according to where we had been housed.

"North one, northeast one, and northwest one." He told the guards to open the gate and let out everyone who was going to court.

As I walked out, I saw the adult men and women coming out of their blocks. They were also going to court that morning. The officer told everyone to line up against the wall and that he wanted the juveniles and women in the front. After a head count was done, we proceeded on. When I walked past the officer, he looked me in the eyes and told me good luck. I wasn't sure if he really meant it, but I told him thanks.

We were taken to a part of the jail known as R&D, which is short for receiving and discharge. This is the gathering place for all inmates coming in and going out of the facility. While walking down the long hall, I saw a few people I knew, but I wasn't in the mood to talk. The only thing I had on my mind was the trial, my life, and freedom. The previous week, a few juveniles who caught murder charges came back from sentencing, and each one of them received life. I didn't want that. I had no control over what was about to take place, and that's what scared me the most.

In R&D, the women were separated from the guys and placed in a holding cell. The other juveniles and I were placed in a cage, and the adult men were put in their own cage as well. Once we were settled in, Tim and I talked about our case, what our lawyers had discussed with us and our defense. I told him we'd be okay, but we had to stay strong. I knew we were fighting an uphill battle, but I tried to stay optimistic. We reminisced and joked around until one of the COs told us that the marshals were pulling up and that we needed to use the bathroom and get ready for transport. I fired up another cigarette, calmed my nerves, and gathered my thoughts.

The back door of the jail swung open, and I saw about ten marshals walk through. A few of them were carrying crates. When they dropped those crates down to the floor, there was a loud thump. They were filled with shackles and handcuffs, so their weight caused them to land hard and fast. The marshals made the announcement that when our name and number were called, we were to step forward and get in line. It seemed like forever, but my name was finally called. I was placed in handcuffs and shackles. After everyone was restrained, we headed outside to the bus and took the short ride to the courthouse. When we stepped outside, the wind hit me hard, and chills went through my body from the cold air.

On the way there, I gazed out of the bus window and watched the people in DC's morning traffic. We rode near the White House, the U.S. Capitol, and other major landmarks in the city that I could see in the far distance. I zoned out and tried to take my mind off the trial. After the twenty-minute ride was over, we were led off the bus like cattle and immediately placed in a holding cell. My friend noticed that I wasn't really focused and told me that I needed to snap out of it. I was in my own little world until I heard the marshal call my name.

"Eddie Ellis," he shouted.

My mom had brought me dress clothes so that I would look presentable in court, so he called me to give me the items. I didn't feel that it was necessary to dress up because, in my mind, the jury knew that I was in jail and that the nice clothes were to try to influence their opinion of me. I was more concerned with them knowing I was innocent and acting in self-defense. 'The guy pulled out a gun first. I feared for my life, so I shot him,' is what I planned to tell everyone. As I thought about what I was going to say, it brought tears to my eyes because I didn't want to be responsible for killing anyone.

The first day of the trial was very stressful, and on top of that, I was so nervous. I knew the severity of my actions, and I also had many friends who'd received lengthy sentences for murder and other crimes. The district attorney started off the trial with his opening argument. His sole job was to prove that I didn't act in self-defense. He painted a picture of me being a cold-blooded killer who was actively looking for this guy to cause him harm. I didn't agree with a lot of the things he said about me or the situation in general, but there wasn't much that I could say. I knew it would be up to my lawyer to rebuff and counter all his arguments.

When it was finally my attorney's chance to speak, I shifted in my seat, anxiously waiting to hear what he had to say. "This was clearly a case of self-defense," was the theme of his argument. "The deceased pulled out a weapon on my client and his codefendant. Therefore, that is self-defense for self and others, not murder." He also talked about the circumstances leading up to the shooting, and how it was a coincidence that the deceased and I ended up at the same party. "My client didn't stalk this guy," he said. "He had no idea who was going to be at that party." At the time, I really didn't understand law and a lot of the language that was being used. But I did know that if someone pulled a gun out on you, then you had the right to defend yourself.

After my lawyer finished giving his opening argument, my codefendant's lawyer spoke. "My client was with Mr. Ellis, and when they came out of the building, my client and Mr. Ellis saw the deceased and his friends standing outside the apartment building. The deceased asked, 'Where is my fucking gun?' My client offered him a gun to replace the gun that was being talked about, and then the deceased pulled out a gun. Mr. Ellis pulled out his gun to defend himself and my client. He discharged the weapon; the deceased was hit and later passed away."

After he was finished, the prosecutor began calling witnesses to the stand. The police officers who arrived on the scene were called first, and they really didn't have any pertinent information to give because they weren't present when the shooting occurred. They gave statements about what witnesses told them. A lot of that information turned out to be untrue. One person said I had a full beard and was about 180 pounds. Another person said they'd known me since I was a kid, but I had no idea who that person was. There were just a lot of things being said that didn't make sense to me. The medical examiner also took the stand and gave testimony about how the victim died. He stated that the cause of death was from a single gunshot wound to the neck.

Our lawyers cross-examined everyone and countered some of the testimony by the police officers, but on the second day of trial, I felt like my lawyer didn't fight enough for me.

Witnesses for the prosecution were called to the stand, and they lied. "No one took a gun from near the victim's body," is what one of them said. I was sitting there thinking that if no one took his gun, then how did it disappear? One of the officers read a statement from a witness that said someone grabbed something silver near the victim and then ran away. There were times during the trial that I would lean over and ask my lawyer to ask a certain question or scribble something on a notepad and slide it to him. Sometimes, he obliged and asked the question, and sometimes he didn't. The prosecution finally rested its case, and I really didn't have a good read on whether I was winning or losing.

On the third day of the trial, I took the stand, and my codefendant did as well. I remember sitting up there telling myself to just tell the truth and everything would be okay. My lawyer asked me what happened on that fateful night, and I told him exactly how it happened.

"My friend and I hooked up and decided that we were going to go to a party. Once we got to the apartment where the party was supposed to be, we found out that it had been canceled. We turned around and left out of the building and were confronted by the victim. He asked for his gun, and we told him that we didn't have it. My codefendant tried to give him another gun. He stated that he didn't want that gun and reached for his weapon. I pulled out my gun, shot him, and then ran."

It was tough being up there on the stand, telling that story to a room full of people. I looked out at the crowd and saw my mother and grandmother. I looked over at the victim's loved ones as well. I had a lot of mixed emotions, but believe me; I was remorseful.

During cross-examination, the prosecutor tried his best to make me mad and get me out of character. It was like a game of cat and mouse, because it seemed like he was trying to catch me in a lie, which was impossible because my story never changed from the time, I was initially detained to the time that I took the stand.

"Well, if he pulled a gun on you prior and made threats, why didn't you call the police?" he asked.

"That's just not the way things are handled where I come from," I said. "When you're in the streets, you don't call the police for a situation like that."

"So, you didn't really feel he was a threat if you didn't call the police for help," he said. "That is what someone who felt their life was in danger would do." He went into a whole spiel about how my codefendant and I conspired to kill the victim on that day. He pushed me to my limit with some of the things that he said, but I remained calm.

My codefendant also took the stand, and his story was the same as mine. We never denied that I shot the guy, but we asserted that it was done out of self-defense.

In 1992, I was found guilty of manslaughter, carrying a firearm without a license, and assault with a deadly weapon. In March 1993, months later, I was sentenced.

"I'm sentencing you to twenty-two years," is all I heard the judge say. My ears went deaf, and tears started to roll down my face. I was distraught. I couldn't even look out in the seats at my family. I couldn't believe what had taken place. I didn't know what my family was thinking or how they felt, but I was devastated. My codefendant was sentenced to twenty-three years under the same charges, but he received an extra year because they charged him for being caught with a gun. I was sentenced under the guidelines of the Youth Rehabilitation Act. Enacted in 1985, one of the purposes of the YRA is to separate youth offenders from older inmates. In other words, I could not be housed with grown men twice my age. The act would also give me the opportunity to have my criminal record sealed at some point. At the time I was sentenced, I had no idea what the act was all about. No one ever took the time to explain it to me. After court, I went back to my cell in the juvenile block in the DC Jail, laid in my bed and cried. I was crushed. I knew that I was going to be in prison for a very long time.

PART

two

Prison

That same year I was sent to the Lorton Reformatory Prison in Lorton, Virginia. The prison was built for DC residents and was operated by the DC Department of Corrections. It was in Southern Fairfax County, VA, about thirty to forty-five minutes from DC. It was opened in 1910 and was known for having deplorable conditions. The complex consisted of approximately seven compounds: Big Lorton, which included the modular intake unit, the Wall – a maximum security compound, Occoquan – the medium-security prison, a minimum-security prison and two Youth Centers that were down the road. I was housed in the youth center part of the facility, but this was an adult prison with a lot of gladiator activity going on. It was ten times worse than the DC Jail. In that facility I witnessed countless beatings, stabbings, and corruption. But I was still happy to be close to home so that my family could come and visit me.

By this time my mother had another son named Emmanuel. I was already worried that my little brother Eric, who was ten years old, wouldn't remember me. Now, the thought that this new little brother would never get to know me really hurt. Family always meant a lot to me, but to my surprise, some of my family members didn't share the same sentiment. A few of them turned their backs on me. They wouldn't accept my phone calls or write me back when I sent them letters. It was a painful time in my life. I couldn't understand why they acted that way. Now I can see the stress I put on everyone, but as a kid, it was difficult for me to see things from their perspectives.

The good part was that my mother, grandmothers, aunts, uncles, cousins, best friend and a few others supported me enough to keep me in good spirits. Maybe that's why I have such love and respect for women. While at Lorton, I began writing, and I expressed myself like I never had before. Writing kept me sane. It was an outlet for me. It helped me maintain my caring side. A side that I couldn't show to other inmates. Writing letters to different women in my life – like my mother, grandmothers and aunts and especially my best friend, Kia – helped me forge a bond with them like I never had before.

I often asked the women I wrote to, 'what does it take to be a man?' I wanted to get their perspective as I was still trying to figure it out. In doing so, I learned that women are way stronger than men. Being in prison showed me that a woman can put up with so much more than a man. A woman can be at her weakest point and still be stronger than a man is at his strongest point. I went into prison as a boy and didn't have much understanding of the dynamics of a woman. I knew them physically, but being in prison helped me to appreciate the love a woman shows not only to men, but to people in general. My mother never left my side, despite the fact that I'd put her in massive debt with lawyer fees. She, along with my grandmothers and aunts, gave me the strength to carry on. They visited me frequently, and we'd just sit and talk for hours. Sometimes they would cry, and sometimes I would as well.

I would like to share something I wrote while I was at Lorton in dedication to the special women in my life.

The Woman

Why is she so special? The woman is the pathway to life. She is the mother of the earth. She is strong. She is loving in her own ways. She is supportive. She is caring. She is beautiful. She is educated. She is a mother, a sister, a grandmother, a cousin, an aunt, a friend, a wife, a girlfriend. I believe the world cannot make it without a woman. I'm not just saying that because babies come through a woman, but because women make life much easier for us men in the world. I would like to take sex out of the picture for a minute because, to me, a woman means more to life than sex.

Besides God, I believe women are the next best comforters in life because they offer us so much mental and emotional comfort, and are always there for us even when we don't deserve them. Women have stood beside us since the beginning of time, even at our lowest points. We need to love them, stand by them, respect them, support them, listen to them, comfort them, and encourage them. I believe that we as men need to stop competing with our women and be happy for them. We shouldn't be ashamed if our women make more money than us.

I believe that women are much stronger beings than men and can bring the best out of a man. I believe that both men and women just want to be loved, cared for, and respected. But sometimes we men become our own foes. Many of us won't open up and receive the love that someone has for us. We allow our fears to hold us back. We are afraid to let someone love us the way they could because we don't want to be hurt. However, when we do that, we miss experiencing the love that we can give and receive. If you are able to open up and love someone, then cherish that feeling. It is a wonderful thing.

Although I explored my caring side through writing, I was still trapped in a violent, vicious environment. I had been locked up for three years. I wrote to my family and friends all the time, and this helped, but remembering the fun times we spent together when I was free often made me break down and cry. I thought about the dreams I gave up to involve myself in the streets. I had always been a talented athlete and wanted to play in the NFL or NBA. I knew if I made it, then I could change the lives of my family. I thought about my freedom. Even though I didn't know how many years I had left to serve, I had not been sentenced to life, so I had light at the end of the tunnel. I wanted to better myself and build on myself as much as I could, so I made sure I was a part of any programming that was available to us. I stayed busy playing basketball, going to my typewriter repair class, and working out.

Then, one day in 1994, a couple of guys and I were gambling, playing spades. They were cheating, giving each other signals, and I caught on to it. While we argued, I reached down in my sock to pull out the knife I'd made. Then I punched the guy sitting to my right in the face. He was already leaning back in a chair, so when I hit him, the chair fell backward, and he hit his head on the ground. The other guy swung, but when he did, I stabbed him in his arm and chest. Once the other guy got up, I stabbed him in the arm also and in the back of the head. The guards heard the fight and ran into the room. The guard grabbed the knife while it was in my hand, but I yanked it, and it sliced his hand open. After that, the other guard tackled me, and I was subdued.

I was not remorseful about what I had to do at that moment because the environment there could be such a dog-eat-dog world. I felt I couldn't allow them to get away with what they did. The truth is that I wish that I didn't feel I had to respond the way I did, but if I hadn't, I felt I would have been creating a bad situation for myself by letting them get one over on me.

After the stabbings, I was locked down and sent to the MAX, which is a maximum-security unit in youth center one. As I walked into the unit, I heard a few friends calling my name and asking me what had happened. I said I would catch up with them later and let them know. The correctional officers walked me down the tier to where the cells were. I had on handcuffs, belly chains, and leg irons, and the chains I had on my legs made that dreaded sound as the metal leg irons scraped the floor as I walked towards the cell. One of the officers called out, '*Open-cell 15.*' The cell door opened, and I was placed inside.

The officer called out, '*Close cell 15,*' and the heavy cell door slammed shut with a loud thundering sound of metal colliding. One of the officers asked me to back up to the cell door so that he could remove the belly chains and leg irons, and then they took off my handcuffs. They handed me a write-up/incident report because of the stabbing that took place and told me that I was to see a disciplinary board in seven days or less but I might also be charged in a street court because of the incident as the two guys I had stabbed wanted to press charges against me.

I walked to the bed and sat down when I heard someone say, "E, come to the vent." I stood up on the toilet so that I could get close to the vent, and heard a voice say, "What's up, E? This is Mike."

Mike was a childhood friend who I had played football with at number 9 Boys and Girls Club. He asked if I needed anything, and I told him to send me some soups, cupcakes, cigarettes and chips. We talked for about ten minutes, and he asked me whether I needed a knife. I told him yes! There were a lot of crazy things taking place in prison, and one had to find a way to protect themselves by any means necessary.

I told Mike that I was going to clean my room and lay back until dinnertime. I jumped down off the toilet and went to the front of my cell, and called for the guy that was on detail. The detail people are the guys who clean up the unit, pass out the food and things like that, but they also help those of us behind bars pass things from one person to the next, and let us know when the correctional officers are close by.

The guy on detail came down to see what I wanted, and I told him I needed some cleaning supplies. He asked if he could get it to me after dinner because, at that moment, the truck was bringing the food down the hill to us. In Youth Center One, the main kitchen would cook the food and then drive food trays to the Max and Three Tower where people were being held in solitary confinement. (Three Tower was under a guard tower and was a very small unit with eight cells in it. By court order, a person could only spend sixteen days at a time there.) I heard the van stop, and the correctional officer Big G opened the front door of the unit, and counted out the trays before the van made its food tray run to Three Tower.

He yelled down the tier, saying that he was going to make his four-p.m. count and then let detail out to pass out the food. Big G opened the gate and walked down the tier to make his count, and as he got to my cell, he said, "E, I will get your personal property to you after count."

I heard the cell doors open for the two guys that were on detail, and one of them came down to my cell and told me that Mike was going to send some stuff over for me after dinner. I told him, thanks!

As the detail guys prepared to bring down the dinner trays, I could hear people coming to life – talking, passing items – and the place just became lively. The detail guy got to my door with a stack of trays in his hand. I grabbed one from the top and pulled it through the tray slot, and on this day, we had fried chicken, bread, fruit and some corn, along with a carton of juice.

I sat down on the bed with my food tray beside me, and I started to pick at the chicken when I heard Mike's voice come through the vent again. "E, your stuff is on the way!"

I jumped up to the vent and said thanks. Before I could even jump down off the toilet, one of the guys was at my cell door with a large bag of items that Mike had sent me, and I thanked him for bringing it to me. My cell door opened, and Big G said, "E, pull that bag into your room and run up here and get your personal property."

As I walked up the tier past each cell, I saw someone standing there and heard a few good men call my name, asking me did I need anything. I told them that I was okay for now. I got to the front gate where the correctional officers sit. Big G opened the gate with the keys and told me to grab my three bags that were sitting there. I grabbed my bags and headed back to my cell after telling Big G thank you.

I sat back down and started to eat my dinner and, as I ate, I started to think about what had happened that day. I was playing cards (spades), and two guys had tried to cheat on me. Because of all the pain, anger, and trauma I experienced over the years, I took it out on them. It's not what I wanted to do, but what I had to do! I couldn't finish all of my food because my mind was on what had taken place earlier and what might happen now – that I might be charged again, which would add more time to what I already had.

I sat the food tray onto the tray slot and then started to look for a rag and body wash in my bag so that I could start cleaning up my cell. I found what I needed. I wet the rag and added the soap, and started to clean. When I was done, it seemed like two hours had gone by. But I was satisfied with the cleaning. I took all of my things out of my bags and placed them under my bed, in the locker and on the top bunk. I made up my bed, took my shoes off and put on my slippers so that I could relax for the night. I took my Walkman and headphones out and started listening to my mix cassette tape with Phyllis Hyman and Teena Marie on it. It calmed me down and allowed me to relax some, because at that time I knew that there was nothing that I could do about what took place today. I washed my face and brushed my teeth, and laid down for bed as I continued to listen to my music. I thought about writing my mother and telling her about what had taken place, but I really didn't want to disappoint her again with my actions, so I just waited.

As I laid back, I heard someone send a song request to a guy named Tracy. I took my headphones off and listened to the brother drop some tunes. He started to sing song after song, and he did a good job, but after a while I fell asleep. I woke up when I heard someone yell, 'chow time,' which meant it was time to eat. I got up and out of bed to wash my face and brush my teeth, and then I went to the bars to see where the detail guys were. I placed my mirror onto the bars so that I could see down the tier. (This is how we kept an eye on what was going on up and down the tier throughout the day when we were in our cell.)

The detail guy, Bob, came to my cell with the stack of trays in his arms. I grabbed one from the top, and then he went to the next cells down the tier until he was done. As he walked back past, he asked each person if they wanted to go to outside rec. I told him yeah.

After a while, I heard the cell doors start to open up, and then my cell opened up and I walked out and headed to the front of the tier where the door to the rec yard was. When I got to the front gate, the officer searched me for a weapon and said I was okay to go outside. As I walked out, there was still a chill in the air, but the sun was coming through the clouds. I saw about ten other guys in the yard; some were working out on the pull-up and dip bar, some were playing handball, and others were just standing around talking. Three guys I came through the system with walked up to me, smiling with their hands out to shake my hand. I shook their hands, and we started to catch up. I told them why I was locked down, and then we started to walk the fenced-in yard while doing pull-ups and dips every lap that we took!

We were allowed to stay outside for two hours. Finally, an officer called us in, and we headed to our cells to get ready for a shower. As we headed in, the officer told us two cells at a time will be allowed to wash up and use the phone for fifteen minutes.

I got back to my cell and gathered my things for the shower, but I picked up a pen and paper to start a letter to my mother and grandmother to kill time before I was called to take a shower and use the phone. About an hour or so went by until my cell door opened, and I walked down with my shoes on with my towel, extra clothes and shower shoes in my hand. I took my shower and got out to use the phone; I called my mother, and we talked until it was time for me to get off the phone and go back to my cell to lay back.

After a few days, I was called to see the disciplinary board for the stabbing incident. I sat in front of the officers as they asked me questions. I really didn't say too much because I knew I was guilty. They found me guilty and condemned me to a year in the Max and 160 days in Three Tower, where I would have to do sixteen days at a time, come back to the Max Unit for one day and then head back up to Three Tower. I would have to do that same routine until the 160 days were up, and then I would finish the rest of my time in the Max Unit.

I built a work-out routine that I did twice a day. I would get up around six a.m. and start doing push-ups and dips until breakfast came, eat my food, go to the outside rec yard or the inside rec cage and workout there for a few and just play handball, basketball or just walk around talking. In my cell, I would read different books and write letters to my family and friends.

We were not allowed to go to school or anything like that, so I found ways to program educationally on my own. I had different books sent in from my family and friends on different topics, and I would read all that I could. Also, while I was locked down in the Max Unit, I got visits from a few of my family members and friends over the months I was there. That really helped me deal with being held in solitary confinement and the depression that it can bring on at times.

One day I went to the inside rec cage to work out, and while in the cage, one of the other guys started to act crazy – throwing things, spitting on the floor, and running back and forth while people asked him to slow down and be cool. I had my cup on one of the two tables that was in the cage, and he knocked my cup off the table. Without thinking, I jumped on him and started to swing until the four officers came into the cage and pulled me off him. They handcuffed me and took me back to my cell, and told me that a write-up/incident report would be coming my way in the next few days because of the fight. All I said was okay, and went to my bunk to grab a cigarette to smoke. I put a sheet up on the bars from top to bottom and then went to the sink and started to bathe myself because I wasn't allowed to take a shower that day.

The disciplinary board came to see me two days after the fight, and I was found guilty of fighting and given another ninety days in the Max. But this time they told me that they were fighting to get me a non-benefit, which meant they were trying to get me kicked out of Youth Center One and sent over to big Lorton. As a result, I stayed down in the Max from 1993 until 1995 and then was sent to medium/YC-2. But before that, I was picked up by the state of Virginia for the stabbing that took place. I went to court and was charged with mayhem and assault with a dangerous weapon. Twenty-one months were added to my DC sentence.

One of the good things about being in medium security was that most of the guys were older than me. Some of them knew my family, and they guided me in the right direction. They helped me understand what it meant to be a man. Don't get me wrong, some of these guys were as crooked and dangerous as they come, but they had knowledge. I observed them, listened to them, and absorbed what I could. Many of these men were old enough to be my father, and I looked up to a few of them. I was at the age where I was searching to find out what it meant to be a man. At the time, they were the only people I could go to for guidance. In prison, the stereotype is that a man is one who knows how to fight well. Or, a man is one who has all the money and women in the streets. To go even deeper, a man is one who has killed and isn't afraid to kill again. However, the truth is that those are all myths. I knew that. But what I didn't know was what it took to be a man. That is what I wanted to know. I was searching for answers.

My identity was still unknown to me. I didn't know how to make good decisions, be responsible, or stay away from trouble. I was my own enemy at times.

— Youngstown, Ohio

Eventually, DC and Virginia officials decided not to renew the contract to house inmates at the Lorton prison complex. All the inmates were transferred to federal and private prisons across the country. The level and frequency of violence in the prison had made it unsafe for everyone, including the guards. Although this prison was primarily for DC residents, there were out-of-towners who were charged with crimes while in the District. They were also housed at Lorton. This prison was known for violence because the inmates couldn't get along. A lot of the violence that took place in the streets spilled over into the prison, therefore causing different neighborhoods and crews to clash.

In 1998, I was transferred to the Northeast Ohio Correctional Center in Youngstown, Ohio. This is a private prison run by the Corrections Corporation of America. The company is the largest private corrections company in the United States, as it manages over sixty facilities. It was incorporated by three businessmen with experience in government and corrections. CCA has contracts with the Federal Bureau of Prisons, Immigration and Enforcement, and the United States Marshal Service. In 2009, CCA's net income was approximately $155 million dollars. This gives you an idea of how much money is made from the private prison industry. They are not into reform or rehabilitation. They are into warehousing, getting paid and creating a new form of buying and selling bodies. I like to call it modern-day slavery.

The Northeast Ohio Correction Center was a new facility,

so on the surface it looked nice and tidy. But it didn't take long for me to notice the disrespect and hostility the correction officers showed towards the inmates. It was almost as if they were trying to get a reaction out of us. Many of the officers were rude and disrespectful at times and, because of that, a lot of them were assaulted. These were not just white officers but Blacks, Hispanics, and guards of all races. Their behaviors caused a lot of tension between the corrections officers and us. They didn't trust us, and of course, we didn't trust them.

I remember one officer saying, "You all are animals and deserve to be treated as such." Another simply said, "you are the inmates, and I am the officer, so whatever I tell you to do, you better do it."

Many officers were beaten up and hurt because of their actions. Guys would not sit around and be talked to in such a disrespectful manner. The thing that bothered me the most was when the white officers called people *niggers*. It got so bad that some of the black officers started to speak out and confront the white officers about using the word. There were a few officers who were good people, and all they wanted to do was their job and go home to their families. However, the disrespect shown by the rogue guards far outweighed the work of the honorable officers. On top of the general disrespect, since the facility hadn't been operating long, the staff was disorganized and inexperienced, and seemed to have no clue what they were doing.

Despite all the commotion, I continued my routine of working out, writing letters, and reading books, but unfortunately, that didn't keep me out of trouble. Shortly after I arrived, I got into a fight with a white officer who crossed the line. He purposely put his hand in my food and thought he'd get away with it. I walked out into the hallway area where the officers hung out in their station. He was standing there like he had done nothing wrong, and out of anger, I punched him in the face and started beating him. I was sent to 'the hole' – solitary confinement, which was a six by nine space with a bed and a small slot in the door where they passed my food through.

After I got out of the hole, I was moved to another block. There I ran into some people that I knew. Everything was cool for a while until tension started between a few people, and I got entangled in the mess. I'd just seen the parole board and was on my way to freedom when a very unfortunate incident occurred. On February 22, 1998, a guy was stabbed in a cell, and five guys (John, Frank, Ken, David and Charles) plus myself, were locked down and charged with the crime.

My friend Frank and the guy who unfortunately lost his life (who I will call William) had fought each other before in 1989 or 1990 while in the juvenile block. Frank won the fight, so over the years there was some resentment on William's side. Let's be real – no man wants to be on the wrong end of a fight. There were some dudes in the unit who were, behind the scenes, hyping William up and instigating. I tried to calm the situation down but tried to stay clear of all the drama because I was headed home soon.

On the morning of February 22nd, we ate breakfast in the unit. The morning was like every other morning for me. When the doors to our cells opened, people went to use the phones, shower, and others went to get their food. I went to get my tray and sat down at one of the tables.

As I was eating, I heard Frank say, "If someone picked up my Tupac Machiavelli tape off the table last night, please return it." In my eyes, he was just trying to find what belonged to him.

Out of nowhere, William said, "Fuck you and your tape."

It was the start of a very bad situation. Frank was up on the top tier, and William was on the bottom floor, eating. He got up and went up toward Frank. I ran up to the top tier to break it up, but they kept pushing and grabbing for each other. Eventually, I moved out of the way and allowed them to go into the room to fight, which resulted in the death of William.

He was stabbed while they were in Frank's cell. I found out later it was William that had the knife, and Frank took it from him. I got caught up because I tried to break up a fight.

I had just talked to my baby brother, Emmanuel, on the phone and told him I would be home soon and help him learn to ride his new bike. However, because of what happened between Frank and William, that day was not going to be around the corner. I was charged with murder and spent the next several months trying to beat the charges. I felt like I was being unfairly charged with a murder that I didn't commit and that I had to fight for my life again like I did when I was first locked up. Once again, one of my codefendants was a friend from my neighborhood. I played football at Number 9 Boys and Girls Club with one of them. The other one, David, was a young brother I tried to take under my wing. I tried to keep him safe and away from all the bullshit that took place. I wanted David to do better than I had done in my early years in prison. I wanted him to stay in the education department and away from the negative things.

Two at a time, we were sent to Mahoning County Jail in Ohio to await trial. Ken and David went first. They took a plea deal to obstruction of justice and were given two years each. We wrote back and forth to each other just to see how things were going, and then, a month later, Frank and I were sent to the county jail. When we got there, I sent Frank a note that said there was a lot of loose steel around, like mop ringers and push brooms with metal in them. I told him that I was going to make a knife or two in case we needed them. He told me it wasn't necessary and I should focus on staying out of trouble and getting home. But I was just in the mindset that I was in a new jail and state, and I was going to protect myself no matter what if I had to.

We were held in the hole for weeks and only came out to shower and use the phone.

But after a time, I found a way to get out more. I convinced an officer that I could cut hair, and the officer gave me the position of the unit barber even though I couldn't cut hair. I just cut bald heads and did shape-ups. But more than anything, this was a way to get out of my cell in the hole and get canteen – chips, candy, cookies, stamps and envelopes from people who could go to the jail store.

When I was there, I came across a good guy from Youngstown, Ohio, named Dre. He had met one of my codefendants, Ken, when he came to the jail, and that's how we became cool. We clicked and, over time, developed a good friendship. I didn't deal with many people, but Dre was a down-to-earth dude and a stand-up guy. I met him back in 1998, and he is still my friend to this day.

One day the sheriff came through, and I asked him why I was being held in the hole.

"You have to do something wrong to get there," he said.

"But I haven't done anything wrong in this jail."

"If that's true, then I'll see to it that you are let out." He was a man of his word because two days later I was out of solitary confinement.

I came out of the hole and was sent to the felony unit. I saw some of the people that I met while I was in the hole, and I talked with a few of them. Others I just stayed away from. I just wanted to keep to myself, go through court and head back to the CCA to do my time. Dre was in the unit right next to me, so we used to talk through the door every day. I remember a time when I was waiting to receive some money from my family, but in the meantime, Dre sent me some food to hold me over. That is the type of brotherhood that kept me going when I was in prison. We stayed in that jail for a few weeks before our trial started.

At trial, I was dressed sharply in clothes that my Uncle Willie brought for me (two suits, some dress shoe boots). I was very nervous because I didn't know what was going to happen. Frank and I sat and listened to our lawyers talk with one another. We started to talk with each other about what was going on. By that time, they had dropped the case of John and Ken, who took a plea to two years for obstructing justice. David and Charles took the same plea deal for two years, so Frank and I were the only two going to trial.

The judge came into the courtroom. We all stood up and then sat down after the judge had seated himself. Frank had said at the preliminary hearing that I'd had nothing to do with what took place, and he did again at trial. The judge just looked at him and didn't say anything. From that point on, I knew that it would be a long road for us. Our lawyers started to present their case, and so did the D.A. All the government witnesses told lies in court, and their statements changed over time. The trial lasted about three or four days. Frank and I sat there and listened to all the lies.

Due to a technicality, the case was declared a mistrial. The district attorney's witness (the prison's lead investigator) lied and said that he wasn't doing his own investigation of the crime, but it turned out that he was. Also, the main inmate government witness changed his statement from what he had said when the incident initially happened. At first, he said I had something to do with it, but then he got on the stand and said he was forced to say things that weren't true.

I was relieved because there was a lot of shady stuff going on surrounding the case, and I knew that I hadn't done anything to the victim. But this was a high-profile murder, and it made national headlines. CCA had just opened the prison a few months before this murder took place, and it put a huge black eye on the facility and CCA. There was a lot of pressure on them. They couldn't just allow a man to be murdered in the prison and not get a conviction.

After the mistrial, we were offered plea deals. I didn't have any faith in the legal system. I knew that they would find me guilty based on Frank's and my history. We were both serving time for murder, and we both had records of previous assaults on officers and other inmates. My lawyer suggested that I take a seven-year plea deal that was offered. Frank was offered an eight-year plea. He was already serving life, so the eight years were nothing for him. He was locked up for murder and attempted murder.

I felt that everyone already knew what took place, and the D.A. knew that their witnesses were lying. They wanted a conviction and didn't care if the truth came out or not. While on trial, I overheard the D.A. state they had lost two witnesses. They recanted their statements and said they weren't going to court. They said they feared for their lives and didn't want to be labeled as rats. However, the D.A. planned to use our criminal backgrounds to get a conviction. At that point I knew that I was fighting a long, uphill battle. I decided that it was best to take the seven-year plea. I didn't want to do it, but I had to.

After that, I was upset with myself for a very long time. I had seven years added to my sentence for a crime I didn't even commit. I know that doesn't look good to a lot of people, but I knew in my heart what happened and what didn't happen. The second manslaughter charge really humbled me and sent me into a state of depression. Right before everything happened, I had seen the parole board and had told them that if they let me out, I would go home and be a law-abiding citizen. Instead, I caught a new charge and had to prepare to do another seven years.

I was sent to lockdown immediately. I was held in a part of the CCA prison that was called Supermax – the solitary confinement unit. I was sent there as a form of punishment. Many of the other inmates had been charged with rape, murder, kidnapping, and armed robbery. We were considered extremely dangerous inmates. Therefore, it was determined that we needed to be segregated from other inmates for safety reasons. For me, it was because of the stabbings, manslaughter charge, and my history of violence.

I sat in a cell locked down for twenty-four hours a day

and began to lose my mind. It was pure misery – torture. It felt like the walls were squeezing in on me. I'd been in the hole before, but this was different. I really didn't know who I was anymore. I paced back and forth in my room for what seemed like hours at a time. I read, exercised, and had a strict routine, but I always ran out of things to do. That's when my mind started to play games with me. I often thought about my family and would go through long bouts of depression.

I took a shower twice, sometimes three times a week. I always had to be strip searched before I left my cell and afterwards as well. For showers, I was still handcuffed and shackled. When I washed my body, the metal would cut through the skin on my ankles, and when the soap touched the sores, it would burn. While in the shower, me and the guys would talk and catch up with each other because, throughout the week, we could only talk through cell doors.

I remember one night; I was sleeping when a white officer kicked on my door. I got up to ask him what was going on. He said, "Nigger, you are going to die in jail."

I had just woken up and felt struck by his words. But I was also angry. I remember saying, "If my door ever opens when you are around, you are going to have serious problems with me." I plotted to get this officer for a while, but the opportunity never presented itself. I'm glad that we never crossed paths in a way that I could have put my hands on him. It would've just added to the problems I was already dealing with.

In lockdown, during that time, I cried, prayed, and continued to fight for my life. But I also did a lot of reflecting. The time I spent in lockdown really made me begin to put my life into perspective. I realized that I would have to make some changes in my life if I wanted to become a better person.

In prison and in life in general before this, I was moving so fast that I didn't have time to think about some of the bad choices I made. Now, at twenty-three, being in lockdown gave me the opportunity to look at my life from the outside looking in. I could no longer blame anything on the negative influences surrounding me because I was locked down by myself. I knew that despite the environment I was in, it would be up to me to change my behaviors and the people I hung out with. Around this time, I had a conversation with my mother. She told me that I needed to change my environment. I told her I couldn't change my environment and reminded her that I was in prison. I had nowhere else to go. She responded by telling me that I needed to change the people that I associated with. She told me to change my mindset about how I viewed life.

From that point on, it was like a lightbulb had turned on in my head. For many people, this advice would have seemed like simple common sense, but I'd been locked up for seven years, since I was sixteen. Prison life and making bad choices had become a way of life for me. I realized that I didn't like the person that I'd become. I was finally at the point where I wanted to change, but I still didn't know how to go about doing that. I started to read more books on black history, politics, slavery, etc. I read *The Autobiography of Malcolm X*, *The Martin Luther King Letters*, *The Count of Monte Cristo*, and hundreds more. I also started working on my spirituality because I knew that God needed to play a bigger part in my life.

the Wall

After about a year, I was shipped back to DC Jail, which was a blessing because it allowed me to see a lot of my old friends and family. However, DC Jail was even worse than when I'd left years earlier. There were cockroaches all over the jail, and the food was disgusting. The young guys had turned the jail into a madhouse. Most of them just wanted to do dumb stuff and not make moves that could've helped them progress. But one good thing was that there were also a lot of seasoned old-timers who were being sent back to DC from different prisons. They knew how to do their time the right way. They minded their business, stayed away from trouble, and didn't do a lot of socializing. The younger guys were wild, and that caused a lot of clashes between the old and the young. The dissension ultimately made it bad for everyone.

I stayed there for five or six months, and then I was shipped out to the Maximum-Security Unit back at Lorton, which was called "The Wall." I got the chance to see a lot of old comrades that I hadn't seen in years. We had all been separated. Over the years, some of us had been sent to Ohio, New Mexico, Texas, Florida, Arizona, and other places. It was good to see friends again! I also used to go to the different religious services to meet up with homies that had just come from the streets to find out what had been going on out in the free world and to just catch up.

Once I got settled in six-block after being moved around, my routine was the usual. I worked out, played handball, and continued writing my letters. Playing basketball was also one of my favorite things to do. It wasn't for the faint of heart because it was very physical, and we were our own referees. I really enjoyed it because I got the chance to let off a lot of steam and frustration when I was playing.

Although a few years had passed, Lorton was still as dangerous as ever. Many people were attacked while wearing handcuffs, and quite a few people were killed behind The Wall. Dudes would pop out of their handcuffs and stab someone in the blink of an eye. The thing about prison is that you had to get your enemy whenever you could catch them.

I had frequent visits from my family, but I had to wear shackles, handcuffs, and a belly chain. That was frustrating. The visits were held in trailers, and I really looked forward to them, despite all the restraints on my body. It felt good to laugh, smile, and touch my loved ones. Their visits got me through some tough times. My mother always encouraged me to stay strong, stay out of the way, and to pray. She knew that I was in a hostile environment, but she also knew that I could make it through.

On one occasion, Grandma came to see me, and we had a good visit. But before the visit was over, she said, "Eddie, I can't do this anymore."

"What, Grandma?" I asked, confused.

"Come to jail to visit anymore. I can't do it." She'd come to see my uncles in prison since the seventies, and now she was tired and burned out. I will never forget that moment. It made me realize the hurt I caused her.

I had joined the Moorish Science Temple of America in 1995, but I really got involved when I decided to change my life. I met a lot of positive brothers and learned a lot of things from them. The temple was a place where people went to try to change their lives and just be better people. We spoke and learned about ourselves, our history and the power of God. They helped me become the man that I am today. I had always read the Bible and other books about God, but the temple helped me study the Christian faith even more. During that transition, I felt spiritually stronger and closer to God. My sense of discernment was heightened, and I was happier.

It was behind The Wall that I realized I had to make better decisions about the people I associated with. I stopped hanging around negativity and chose to hang around individuals who were living the way I wanted to live. I explained to a lot of my friends that I was trying to change. That was a hard thing to do. When I sent letters and notes to a few people about my change and what I wanted to do, some of them got mad. Others were okay with it, but at the end of the day, this was for me and not for them. I learned that true friends want to see you do good despite what they're doing. I was being real with myself finally, and that's all that mattered to me.

The charge that I caught in Ohio was an eye-opener, and I was determined not to get in any more trouble. At this point in my life, I was twenty-three years old and still struggling to figure out what it took to be a man. This was a recurring thought that I had in prison. I really wanted to know. Then, one day while sitting in my cell, it hit me. A man is someone who is responsible, independent, caring, respectful, and loving. I had never made those characteristics a part of my life. As time went on, I realized that this was the kind of person that I wanted to be, and those were the types of people that I wanted to have in my circle.

Even though I decided that I was going to become a better person and do the right thing, the reality was that I was still in prison and staying safe was my biggest concern. Prison is a place where, in one moment, everything could be peaceful and then, out of nowhere, there could be an all-out war going on. I was concerned over the fact that some people took offense that I had started to see life and myself in a different light. I wasn't scared, but I had to keep an edge that would allow me to protect myself. Prison is not a place for the weak, so someone who showed emotion or carried himself in a certain type of way could become a target.

Change in my life didn't come easy. It didn't come overnight, either. It was a painful process. I learned that it didn't make me less of a man to cry. I sat in my cell many nights and cried. I thought about my past. I thought about my family, whom I missed a lot. I regretted the choices that I'd made. I thought about the people I'd hurt, the opportunities that I lost, and my dream of being a professional athlete. It was a hell of a reality to know that I could have done so many different things with my life. Instead, at night I slept in a cold and dark prison cell.

The Dandelion

The Dandelion is something that is better known in the hood as the buttercup. When I was seventeen and eighteen locked up in prison in Lorton, I was trying to figure out how I was going to make it through the twenty-two-year prison sentence that was given to me. I used to look out of my window and daydream about my freedom and my childhood, family, and friends. While looking out of the window at the sky and grass outside, I would also always see many tiny yellow flowers out there, which my friends and I used to call buttercups when we were young. When I got to go outside, I used to walk around the prison ground and see these flowers growing through the cracks in the ground, in the side of the road, and in the dirt.

As the years went by, I learned this flower was really called a dandelion. I've never seen another flower grow in many places like the dandelion did. Some people call it a weed. This so-called weed is a pest to most people because it's not a fancy flower like the rose, tulip, lily, or other fancy blossoms. To some people it just interferes with their lawn or garden. But, for some reason, as a kid, I liked to play with the dandelion (or, to me, the buttercup). I would put it under the chin of a girl and say that she had sunshine under her chin. Sometimes the girls

64

*would put the buttercups behind their ears and in their hair.
They looked so pretty to me when they did that. Again, it may
be a weed to many, but no matter what, for me, it will always
stand out because it's beautiful.*

*I don't know too much about flowers, but I do know that
those so-called fancy flowers can't grow in the many places
that the dandelion can. When I see the dandelion today, I see
strength and beauty. When I was at Lorton. I told myself that if
the dandelion can grow in dirt and unrich soil, then I can grow
inside these prison walls and become a better man despite the
dehumanizing circumstances. I began to think of the dandelion
as an inspiration and model for myself and others in prison
and outside. Black men and women have been through so much
in their lives, but they still survive and even can thrive despite
their circumstances. We have all been called a name one way or
another, just as people say the dandelion is just a weed. Nevertheless, a dandelion never stops growing through the cracks in
the concrete. So we can do the same –stand up and get ready to
grow in unrich places, to become beautiful people with strong
characters.*

*If you go to a park in the summertime, stand in the grass,
close your eyes, and then open them. The dandelion will stand
out like it's saying, "Look at me."*

Red Onion

The year was 1999, and I was still in two-block behind The Wall. One night around one a.m. I was laying on my bunk in my cell listening to Phyllis Hyman, "Meet Me on The Moon," and that's where my mind was. Phyllis Hyman's voice is so relaxing to me. Suddenly I heard the rattle of a lot of keys and loud voices. I jumped up out of my bunk and put my mirror onto the cell bars so that I could look down the tier to see what was going on. I noticed a lot of officers gathering, so I made sure my cell was clean from things that were considered contraband; then I lay back on my bed till I heard one of the officers' yells, "If you hear your name called, pack up your things because you are being shipped out."

I'd seen many people get shipped to different places over the past few months because DC was still closing its prisons. By that time, Lorton had only one prison open, which was the max unit, and the other five prisons were closed. I heard about ten people get their names called, and a few of them were my friends. A couple of them called my name and asked me to call their mother, wife, or girlfriend. We always had a system in place to let our loved ones know if we were ever shipped out. If you didn't have someone to call and let them know, then there's no telling when they would find out.

We never knew when our name and number would be called to be shipped out, but when we heard people being called, we were on edge. I wanted to stay close to home as long as I could because I was able to see my family and friends during visitation. If you're sent across the country, then it's difficult for loved ones to make the trip to visit.

My name wasn't called that night, so I felt relieved. I continued my routine as much as possible as far as working-out, playing basketball, handball, writing, reading, etc. But to be honest with you, it didn't feel the same to me because I knew that sometime soon, my name would be called, and I would be on the road headed to another facility. On that weekend my childhood best friend Boo was back in town, and she came to see me. She had been living in Hawaii, where she was stationed in the military. I hadn't seen her in years, but she had been by my side throughout my time. She had supported me the best way that she could. I am forever grateful for her friendship.

Then it finally happened. Early one morning I was woken up by an officer. He told me that I was being shipped out in a few hours. I asked him if I could use the phone to inform my mother that I was being moved. He said I had five minutes to take care of that and opened my cell door. I walked down to the phone and dialed my mother's number. As the phone rang, I just thought about where I was headed. My mother answered, and I told her that I was being shipped out of town again, and that this may be my last time until I was released. I couldn't tell her where I was going because I didn't know. She told me that she loved me and that I needed to stay away from trouble if I ever wanted to come home. I said that I would and that I had to go.

When I got back to my cell, I started to pack my things. Some of the stuff I couldn't take with me, so I passed them down to a friend of mine. Most of the time when people were moved, they'd leave stuff for friends. That day I left a radio, some magazines, some of the snacks I had and a few other things. But I took all my books, legal and regular mail, pictures and clothes with me.

When I finished packing, I called the officer and told him that I was ready to go. He said that he was still waiting for the call to let him know that they were on the way to get me and the others. I heard people from other blocks in The Wall yelling that they were being shipped out as well. Those were always crazy moments, I think, because people wanted to stay close to home so they could see their loved ones.

A few minutes later, my cell door popped open. When I came out, the officer said I could walk around until they came to get me. I walked to my friend's cell and talked to him about all the moving that was going on. Thirty minutes went by, and finally the officer told me they had arrived and were ready for transport. I thanked him for the phone call and went back to my cell to gather my belongings.

I grabbed my things, walked down the tier and told the men to stay strong and keep their heads up. I went to the top of the tier, and the officer put the belly chain on me, then the handcuffs, and then the shackles. We headed outside. The cold air was blowing, and all I was thinking about was staying warm and where I was headed. One of the officers grabbed my property, and we started to walk. Once I got outside of Two Block, I saw people being walked out from Four Block and Six Block. When we met up, there were about twenty people being moved. We headed to R&D, talked amongst ourselves and waited to be checked out.

In R&D, we were checked out and then told to get in a straight line and move forward. We were loaded into vans and once again packed in like a herd of cattle. It's hard to feel like a human being when you have no control over your life and are treated like this. Being shipped out was always stressful. It wore on me. I was in one place one year and in another the next. I had no control over my life.

As we were being herded into the vans, I asked one of the officers where we were being shipped to. He told me Red Onion. I was glad to know my next destination. I didn't want to be surprised. A lot was going on in my mind.

Red Onion State Prison was a Supermax facility in Pound, Virginia. It was new, as it had just opened in 1998. It was a level six segregation facility, and I knew I would once again be locked down twenty-three hours a day, seven days a week. I had a few friends who were in Red Onion, and they had written me about the jail. I'd also always heard rumors about the place. I was told about the racist officers who tried to inflict fear into people with threats. I heard about the intimidation and scare tactics they used against new inmates. I was prepared for all of this because I'd experienced the same behaviors throughout my time in DC Jail and the CCA prison in Ohio. By that time, I knew how the correction officers operated. Most of them just talked a lot of trash.

Driving to Red Onion was a long and grueling ride. I was in handcuffs, had a belly chain wrapped around me, and shackles on my feet. I talked with others in the van for a little while, but I eventually went into a zone and stared out of the window. I had to mentally prepare myself for what lay ahead.

Finally, the van pulled up to a road and drove up to the prison. There were a lot of trees in the distance behind it. However, the prison took the beauty away from them. Prisons are so destructive and block the nice scenery of the things around them. This place was grim. After the officer called everyone's name, we got off the vans one at a time and formed a line. We were all lined up near a wall, and over to my left all I could see were black bodies with chains on them. I saw about ten white officers barking orders at us, and a few of them were holding shotguns and sticks.

The officer that was in charge started to talk to us in a very threatening and disrespectful way. He told us if we didn't listen to him, then there were going to be problems. I blocked him out because I didn't want to hear what he was saying. I'd seen that whole song and dance before. The only thing I wanted to hear was what unit I was going to. I was tired and needed some sleep. The officer started calling names again, and this time he told us to get into three different lines. I was put into the first line. Once we were lined up, we were ordered to follow him.

We went to R&D to get our bedroll, which was the sheets and our blanket. The officer went over the rules and personal things that we could and couldn't bring with us. They let us keep soap, toothpaste, socks, boxers, tee-shirts and a religious book. They told us we would get our other belongings later in the week. I was taken to a familiar place, the hole. Out of the twenty people that came with me to Red Onion, only two of us were placed in the hole. On the way, I asked the officer why I had to go. He said that it was because of my history of violence. I shook my head and kept walking. We arrived at the unit, and the officer yelled to the officer in the booth to open the gate. He told him that he had two troublemakers for him. We walked into our cells, and the cell door closed behind us. We were told to put our hands out of the tray slot so that they could take the handcuffs off. Then they took the shackles off as well.

Once I got in there, I unpacked and placed my things on shelves and tables. Then, I grabbed a tee shirt and ran water on it along with some soap because I wanted to clean the place. They usually do a poor job of doing that, if they even bother to do it at all. I washed my sink very well and then started on my mattress, the walls, the toilet and the floor. After that, I made up my bed and laid down to rest. I was so sleepy I dozed off in no time. It felt like I was asleep for hours, but it was only an hour or so before I heard someone knocking on my door telling me it was lunchtime. I went to the door and heard people talking. Someone said that some new people had come in from Lorton. I didn't say too much because in Lorton many of us were enemies, and I just wanted to lay low.

The food slot opened, and I grabbed my meal. The dude that brought the food to my door looked up and started to smile when he saw me. I did the same thing because he was a good guy that I hadn't seen in years. We were in Oak Hill together as kids back in 1991.

"Eddie E, what's been up, Slim?" he yelled. "It's been a while since I've seen you."

"Dave, I haven't seen you in so long, but what's been up?" I said. We caught up for a little while, and then the officer told him to continue passing out food trays and head back to his unit. But before Dave left, he told me he would get me a bag of things together and send them over to me later in the day.

I laid back down to relax, and then I heard someone call my name. I went to my door again to look out of a slit of glass. I was trying to figure out who was calling me. It was a guy named Eric. We talked at the door for an hour or so. We talked about the people in Red Onion and who was still in Lorton when I left. As the day went on, I talked to and caught up with a few good men, and then I heard the speaker box in my cell come on. The officer told me to come to the Bubble (the safety control part of the unit) to get some property. I put my shoes on and walked to get my things. I thought it was the stuff that I had brought with me, but it turned out to be the things that Dave promised me.

I thanked the officer and went back to my cell. I opened the bag and there was some food, snacks, a Walkman radio, a few tapes, some cigarettes, a sweat suit, stamps, paper, and other things. I went through everything and found a note relaying to me what had been going on in the prison. Dave told me who was there when it comes to friends and foes and who to talk with to get out of the hole. It's always good to run into a few good men like Dave, and it was a relief to have some personal property like books to read, a Walkman and tapes, snacks, etc. That night I laid down and tried to rest as much as I could, but I didn't get much sleep.

My food was on the tray slot waiting for me when I got up in the morning. After I was done eating, I washed my face, brushed my teeth, and started to work out. I did pushups, dips, and jumping jacks to get my morning going. As I was working out, an officer came to my door and asked me if I wanted to go to recreation. I told him that I did. I was asked to strip, and I did so with hesitation, because no matter how long I'd been in prison, I still didn't like that. The officer asked me to put my hands through the tray slot. He put on the handcuffs; the door opened, and he placed the belly chain on me with a dog leash on a chain. At that time so much started to run through my mind. I started to change my mind and tell him to put me back in my cell. However, I needed to go out and see who was there and who I could talk with about the stuff that I needed. While I was being walked to the cage, I asked the officer who I could talk with about getting into population. He told me that I was on the list to be seen by prison officials.

When I got to the cage, I saw some dudes that I knew and some who I'd never seen before. I was placed into the cage, and the officer took the handcuffs off and then the belly chain. I was in a single-man cage, but I was still able to talk to my friends. I asked them if there was anyone in the prison I knew, and they asked me about people we were locked up with in Lorton. One of my homies told me to be careful with some of the officers because they were racist.

My friends and I talked so much that the hour of recreation went by fast. As I was leaving, one of the officers came to me and said that I was scheduled to see the unit manager and counselor before I went back to my room. I was cool with that, but I knew they were going to talk with me about my violent history. I also knew they wanted to talk to me about the witnesses from the case in Ohio who were also in the facility. Some of my codefendants were also in Red Onion, and they didn't want us talking, or around one another because of the past trouble we'd gotten into. I knew they would also want to know about guys I'd stabbed and others I'd gotten into fights with. But I just wanted to be with some friends, play some cards, use the phone, and play dominos.

When I got to the office, I was surprised. I immediately sat down. I was surrounded by three officers, a unit manager, and a counselor. They asked for my DC number, and then the unit manager and counselor told me that my prison jacket (record) hadn't arrived yet. Therefore, they allowed me to go to open population. I gladly thanked them and was taken back to my cell. I didn't worry too much about my safety, even though Red Onion was a high-level max prison. I wasn't scared and felt I should've been able to go to their open population block and move around freely. I was done with getting in trouble. It felt so good when the handcuffs and belly chain were finally removed. After that, I sat down in my cell and relaxed until lunch. I still remember having a hamburger, fries, a cookie and corn. I'd stopped eating red meat by that time, so I just took the bread and made a peanut butter and jelly sandwich.

After about an hour, an officer came to my door and told me that I would be moved to the open population unit after they picked up the trays. I started to pack the little stuff that I had while I waited until the officer came back. He finally called my name and asked me if I was ready to go. He came to the cell, placed the handcuffs and belly chains on me, and my cell door popped open. We walked out to the unit door and waited for it to be opened. I heard a few people saying, "E, I hope to be over there soon."

I told them, "I'll be looking forward to it."

I walked through the unit door and headed to the open population unit. It was what I wanted and had been waiting on. When I got to the unit, they took the handcuffs and belly chain off. I walked into the cell and saw that I had a cellmate, so I placed my stuff down and went right back out to see who it was. I saw many guys that I was okay with, and I went over to them.

"E, what's been up, Slim? Were you in Ohio? Were you in Lorton? Do you need anything?" they wanted to know.

I answered their questions, but my main concern was who I was going to be in the cell with. The dude was playing cards and not really paying attention, but one of the guys called him over. I pulled him to the side to see what was up with him as a man.

"What's up, Slim? My name is Eddie, and people call me E. What's your name?" I said.

"Oh, my name is Mike, and I remember you from Ohio."

"Okay," I said. "Do you smoke?"

"Yes. I do," he replied.

"I don't smoke, so do you mind smoking when we are not in the cell together?" I said.

"Oh no," he said. "I respect that, and I will just go into my friend's cell and smoke."

"Thanks, Slim!" I said. That was our first conversation, and over time we had many more. He was a good dude.

A short time later an officer shouted, "Lock down!" We went back into our cells, and all I could hear were doors closing. Some people asked why we were being locked back down.

"Because we can." I heard an officer say.

My cellmate and I began to talk. I mentioned that I couldn't remember where I knew him from. He told me that he saw me on the news in Ohio when I was caught up in the murder in the CCA. We played some spades, conversed and got to know one another. He told me about some of the dudes in the block who were not getting along and what had been going on the past few days. No matter the prison, there was always conflict and different issues going on. From day one I told myself that I was going to stay out of trouble and focus on going home. At the time I wasn't trying to get caught up in any more bull crap.

Later that day we went outside. I talked for a little while, and then I hit the basketball court and did what I did best. I balled out and had some fun. That was something that I hadn't done in a while. After I finished, I talked to a few good men about what had been going on in the prison and where I could get a knife if I needed one. Although I wasn't looking for trouble, there was a lot going on. They told me they'd show me where the knife was stashed later in the day.

The officers yelled that we had to return to our unit, so I gathered all my belongings and headed back. One of my homies said, "E, you have to stay within that line, or they will say that you are out of bounds." I just laughed because through all the jails and prisons I had been in, I'd never heard that before. Then, I heard an officer say, "If you're outside of my lines, you are going to the hole." I just looked at him and shook my head.

When we got back in the unit, one of the officers said that we had thirty minutes to get in the shower and back into the cells. I went to the shower, washed up, and said a few words to the homies. One of them showed me where the knife was stashed. I was good once I saw that. My mind was at ease, and I just wanted to lay down and relax.

My body was killing me because I hadn't played basketball in a long time. I just lay on my bunk and thought about my life and where it was at the time. When I looked back on things, I felt down because I made some very dumb choices along the way. Yet, God still blessed me through it all. I was more responsible, made better decisions, and had a more mature state of mind. Still, I envisioned myself doing so much better in the future. I never lost faith in God, and I finally started to feel like a man.

The cell doors opened, and people started to come out of their cells and line up for chow. When I came out, there was a lot of tension in the air. I hadn't felt it earlier in the day, before I went outside or when I was outside playing ball. I thought to myself, *"Did I miss something?"* I pulled a few guys to the side and asked what was going on. They told me that some dudes got into it before I came, and the beef was back on.

Once we got into the chow hall, people walked through the line to get their food. I got my tray, sat down, and ate for thirty minutes or so. I asked the guys at the table about the make-up of Red Onion. They told me that there were almost 100 guys from DC there, but that there were mostly Virginia guys in the prison. That made sense because we were in Virginia. The problem was that DC dudes didn't really click up and get along with a lot of people. If we weren't beefing with one another, then we beefed with guys from the other states.

When we got back to the unit, I laid low and tried not to pay attention to what was going on around me. I was tired of the drama and just wanted to do my time peacefully. However, when there's that much tension in the air, it's hard to just relax. When we came out from dinner, and when I got close to my cell, I saw two dudes go into a cell, and then the door closed. All I heard was banging on the door and bodies hitting the walls and the floor. It went on for twenty minutes or so, and then it was over. The two guys came out and went their way. I went to the card table and played until we were locked down for the night.

It had been a long day, so I lay down on my bunk and drifted off to sleep. I woke up to the sound of an officer saying that it was chow time and we had to be ready in twenty minutes. I jumped off my bunk, washed my face, and brushed my teeth. The cell doors opened for us to line up, and one of the officers led us down to the chow hall. When we lined up, I noticed that the two guys that fought were not in line with us. People started talking and said that someone had dropped the dime on them. Someone snitched about their fight. We went to the chow hall, and I just chilled and listened to people talk. I kept my opinion to myself. As we were eating, I watched the officers closely and noticed there were more of them in the chow hall than normal. They were on guard because they knew there could possibly be another altercation.

When we finished eating, I heard one of the officers say, "Wrap it up, take your trays and line up." People started to line up, and I overheard one of the officers say it was a fight in one of the cells and they were going to see if more people were involved. I walked by and looked in the other direction because I didn't feel like going through the bull crap with anyone that day. As we piled back into the unit, we started to talk, and some people went to the card table. I looked in the cell where one of the dudes that was in the fight had been, and the cell was empty. Both had been taken to the hole.

I was in chill mode, so I played a few hands of spades, and then I started doing pull-ups and walking around. At times I loved being by myself and not paying attention to all the riff raff. That stuff can be so time-consuming. A few hours went by, and then it was time to go out to the rec yard. I was happy because I could play basketball and burn off some stress.

While I was playing ball, I saw the door to the building open. Everyone on the yard took notice of that. Six officers came out of the door; four of them were in swat uniforms, which meant something was about to go down. I wasn't worried about anything because I hadn't done anything wrong. But, as I started to dribble the ball, I heard my name called.

I turned around and said, "What's up."

One of the officers said, "Come with us."

"For what?" I said.

"Mr. Ellis. Come with us, please."

I hesitated before I walked over to them, and before I got there a few of my homies said, "What's going on? He didn't do anything. He just came here."

One of the officers said, "We just need to talk with him."

I walked over to them, and they placed the handcuffs and the belly chain on me. My mind was running wild because I really hadn't done anything wrong, and I was trying to figure out why they had come to get me.

I heard my homies say, "This is messed up. We are going to find out what's going on, E. Don't even worry about it."

I walked with the officers and didn't say anything to anyone because I was sick and tired of being locked down for bull crap. I walked into the unit manager's office, and I was told to take a seat. I sat down.

The unit manager said, "Mr. Ellis. Your jacket came in from

DC. We didn't know that you had assaults on officers, other inmates and a manslaughter charge while in prison. You haven't given us any problems since you've been here, but we can't have you in open population with those kinds of write-ups. Do you have anything to say?"

"Well, the assaults on officers and other inmates were years ago, and I was defending myself. As for the manslaughter charge – that was two years ago, and I am living my life in a positive way now."

"Okay. We will review your case in two weeks and see what we can do. I will put a good word in for you, Mr. Ellis."

"Thank you," is what I said, but 'put me back in my cell and leave me alone,' is what I was really thinking.

I was walked to a cell in the hole, and my personal property came later that day. After I had been there a while, I heard something slide under my cell door. It was some notes from my friends asking me what was going on. They told me that they thought my cellmate had gotten me locked down. I sent a note that said it wasn't my cellmate but that my jacket had come in from DC, and they had looked at what I'd done in the past. Just when I thought things were getting better, I found myself back in a familiar place, the hole. My past haunted me again.

For the next week, all I did was work out in my cell. I had limited contact and communication with others, so I had no other choice. I also worked out when I was in the outside cage. For the rest of my time there, I wrote letters and listened to Scarface and the Ghetto Boys on my Walkman. I thought about my past and my future. I thought about all the trauma that I went through and all the violence I'd been a part of over the years. Up to that point in my life, I'd felt like a failure. But I also began to think about wanting to get out of prison and help folks who were locked up and those coming home. I stayed positive the best I could during the three to four months I spent in Red Onion. Then, one morning I heard a loud bang on my cell door, so I got up. The officer told me to pack my stuff. I was being transferred.

Alcatraz *of the*
─────────── Rockies

In June 2000, I was sent to Oklahoma City, the Federal hold-over, on my way to the Federal Bureau of Prisons. The hold-over was right on the airport grounds in Oklahoma City. I had no idea what prison I was going to, but this was one of the transit spots for the BOP. The plane ride there was one of the scariest moments of my life. I sat by the window in handcuffs and shackles with a black box over the handcuffs. (The black box is used to go over the top of handcuffs when inmates who they consider high security are transferred from place to place.) The restraints hurt my wrists, and the whole time I was thinking that if the plane were to crash, there would be nothing that I could do to save myself. When we arrived, the plane pulled up to a building at the back of the airport. After the plane stopped, the marshals told us they would start from the front and work their way to the back to let us off. They told us to not get up until we were told to do so.

People started getting off the plane, and all I could hear were chains rattling and orders being barked. After my row was called, I got up and walked down an aisle that seemed two miles long. The chains made it difficult to walk at times, and my legs felt numb from sitting for so long.

As I approached the front of the plane, the marshals told those of us with black boxes on our handcuffs to move to the side. I did just that, and there were two others with black boxes as well. One of the correctional officers came up to me and said, "You are back in my jail, and you are going to have problems this time."

"You've got me confused," I replied. "I've never been in your jail."

However, he was very adamant that I was the person that he was talking about. The other officers seemed to become on guard when the officer kept saying there would be problems. They watched me carefully. The only thing that was running through my mind was that the officer was on some bullshit because he was confusing me with someone else that he had a run-in with in the past. I knew he was attempting to try and strike fear in me, but it didn't work. Before I went up to my cell, he came back and told me that I was right.

"You're not the person I was thinking about," he said.

And I just looked him in his eyes and walked away. Nevertheless, I was placed in the solitary confinement unit and placed on a three-man hold – which means that you cannot be moved without three officers being present.

I stayed at Oklahoma City Federal holdover for about seven days. I couldn't go outside to the one-man cage unless there were three officers to escort me. The food was the worst, but I had to eat to survive. I couldn't order any canteen from the jail, and I wasn't able to use the phone the entire time I was there. I wasn't even given paper and pen to write my family to let them know where I was. The air in the room was extremely cold, and it was hard to stay warm with the thin sheets and blankets that were given to me.

On the third day, I was able to go outside to the one-man cage to work out for an hour. It was around eight in the morning and very chilly outside. I had to work out to stay in shape. That was the best way for me to relieve stress. I did push-ups, jumping jacks, and pull-ups. To do the pull-ups, I put a towel through the cage and then wrapped the towel around my hands. I pulled myself up with my chest scraping up against the cage. After every set, I ran around for a few minutes and then got back to my sets.

One day I was reading a book, and I heard a knock on the wall.

"What's up?" the guy next door said. "Where are you from?"

"That's not important," I replied. I was a bit frustrated and stressed about being moved. I was not in the mood to make any new friends. I went back to reading as I was really enjoying this book. It was a book about the West and the life of Mountain Men and cowboys called *The Mountain Man*. I loved that book because it made me feel like a black cowboy. I'd had the opportunity to ride horses when I was a kid, and reading those books made me think about the outdoors and riding. After that book, I read three other mountain men books. Reading allowed me to escape the reality of being in prison. I'd get so deep into the novels that I'd become a part of the story.

The days went by very slowly in that place. I just wanted to get on to wherever I was supposed to go. Finally, one day I was sleeping when I heard a knock on the door. "Pack your things. You are being shipped out," the officer said.

I jumped up fast because I was ready to go. I didn't have any personal property, so there wasn't really anything for me to pack. When the officers came back, I asked one of them what prison I was going to. He told me he didn't know, but I'd find out once I got there. It felt like forever for the officers to come and get me. When they finally did, I noticed there were more than the three officers that normally took me outside to the cage. I wasn't sure if I was really going to be moved or if they were going to harm me. However, I was taken down to be transported to another prison within the Bureau of Prisons. They put me and about thirty other guys on a bus to be taken to our next destination.

I was given my seat, and as people started to fill the bus, I noticed that I was the only person with a black box on top of my handcuffs. I didn't understand why. It made me feel uneasy. As the bus started to take off, guys started to talk to one another. I stayed to myself because I was just wondering where I was going. Once again, I drifted off into a mental zone as I often did on the bus trips. As we were riding, an older guy three seats back asked the guy behind me to get my attention. I turned around with a look on my face that I didn't want to be bothered because I really didn't. I just wanted to take the ride and get on with my time. I asked the guy what he wanted, and he asked me if I had an uncle named Willie. I asked him why he wanted to know. He told me they were friends. I held a small conversation with him because I really didn't know who he was, and at that time everybody was on the 'can't be trusted' list.

I arrived at The United States Penitentiary, Administrative Maximum Facility, better known as ADX. Located in Florence, Colorado, and approximately 100 miles or so away from Denver, this place is known as the clean version of hell or, better yet, The Alcatraz of the Rockies. The facility was operated by the Federal Bureau of Prisons, better known in the streets as the Feds. It housed 450 inmates who were deemed the most dangerous and in need of the tightest control in the U.S. Federal Prison system.

I was sent there based on my actions in DC prisons and the CCA private prison in Youngstown, Ohio. In Lorton, I was charged with the stabbing of two inmates. I was locked down and taken to court for assault and mayhem. I was found guilty and given eighteen months running with the twenty-two years I was given in DC courts. In the CCA, someone had lost their life, and the officers panicked and started grabbing everyone in sight. They locked up a few people and put them in the hole/solitary confinement. I was one of them. Therefore, I had street and prison charges that reflected a high level of violent tendencies. Therefore, it was determined that I needed to be segregated from other inmates and have tight supervision.

Once we arrived at the penitentiary, almost everyone's name was called except mine. I asked the marshal why my name wasn't called.

"You're going to the big house up the road," he replied.

I had no clue of what he was talking about, but as the last two guys on the bus exited, they told me I was going to Supermax. The bus pulled off, and we headed to a place that I knew was going to be harsh. As I exited the bus, three or four marshals walked me up to the back door, and another four or five correctional officers came out with sticks in their hands. One of them had a camera and took my picture. They walked me into the facility. They stripped me, asked for my DC number, name, date of birth, and a few other questions. After that, I was immediately placed in the hole.

Solitary confinement in ADX was different from others I had been in because there were double sliding doors with bars behind them. My new room was essentially a boxcar cell. The cell was a cage where the top, bottom, back, and sides were all concrete walls. Inside my 12x7 foot cell was a concrete slab that my mattress sat upon. The concrete was solid, and the mattress was as thin as paper. There was a built-in shower that came in handy, but there wasn't much to like about that place.

I didn't know how long I'd be in the hole, but I later learned that I would be locked down anywhere from twenty-three to twenty-four hours every day. The prison controlled all my contact with the outside world. My one phone call per month was monitored, and my food was always hand-delivered by a correctional officer.

The first year there I felt like I was losing my mind. I spent so much time alone that I longed to be able to talk with someone. I was in a very lonely place that was meant to mentally break me down. I kept telling myself that I had to be strong, but the more I did, the weaker I became. I felt like I was fighting a ghost. I hallucinated, had shortness of breath, and was in a mad state of depression. I often heard other inmates screaming, wailing, and banging their heads on the walls.

84

Many inmates attempted suicide by cutting themselves with sharp objects. I even heard stories of people slicing off their ears, removing their testicles, and spreading human waste all over the walls.

A few weeks after I arrived, I was moved to a new unit. I immediately noticed the prison politics between the different races, but I tried not to function like that. I was a very proud black man, and I still am, but I tried to keep hate out of my mind and heart because it's a very powerful force that can be destructive. As soon as I arrived, I got a note from a homie named Gizmo. He told me to be careful with the correctional officers and to watch out for some of the white guys when I go outside. He let me know that the COs put him in a trap a few years back. He said he went on the yard, and the COs had skipped all the black guys' cells but let all the white guys out. He told me that two of the white dudes tried to jump him, and he had to fight them off. One of them cut him with a razor blade, but Gizmo knocked the other one unconscious. Then the COs came out to break it up. There were other guys who told me about situations like that, so I paid close attention to what was going on around me. Whenever I went out of my room, I made sure I was in a situation where I could protect myself.

One day, while I was doing a few one-handed pull-ups, an old racist officer said, "Eddie, you are stronger than I thought."

I jumped down and said, "Try me, and I will show you how strong I really am." I walked around and finished my workout.

Two days later, four COs came to my door and told me to stick my hands through the door to be cuffed.

"For what?" I asked.

"It doesn't matter. Just cuff up." I didn't know what was going on, so I allowed them to put on the cuffs. Once I got out of the cell, they told me that I was being moved because I said I was going to hurt one of the officers.

I was so upset because the only way to get out of this

prison was through the step-down program, which is the unit that allows people to program their way out of the ADX into one of the BOP penitentiaries, a very special order but at least not in a body bag. That was my fourth year in the ADX, and I was ready to get out of that place. After the incident with the racist officer, I was taken to an area in the back of the prison for six or seven months, and then I was able to come back to the step-down unit. I knew many of the people in this block because some of them had been in my block when I was in the back of the prison.

The step-down program was split up into two sides, J-unit and K-unit. I'd been back in the step-down unit for a few weeks, and everything had been going well. There was still tension in the air, but I had gotten accustomed to it. It was wintertime, and it got very cold, both inside and outside. I used to go to the small rec yard that consisted of a half basketball court, a wall to play handball, pull up and a dip bar. They really didn't like for us to go out if the snow wasn't shoveled, so I used to volunteer to do it. For me it was a work-out, plus I wanted to go out and get some fresh air.

I did that for a week or so, and then, one day, this 6⬜white CO guy asked me to put the shovel down and come back inside. I did what he asked me to do. Then he asked me to step into my room, and I did. Next, he came to my door and told me he didn't feel safe around me anymore. I was sent to the back once again. I was very upset because I didn't do anything to that big coward. While in the back, I started to feel like I wanted to do harm to one of the officers. I felt like they were picking on me and getting me moved for no reason.

I knew that I couldn't let them distract me, so I sought ways to grow and not let the hate that was going around affect me. I understood that hate is very powerful, and I really didn't want to be a part of it. There were a lot of people in that prison who didn't like me just because of the color of my skin. I tried not to see color when dealing with people. I treated people a certain way based on how they treated me and others.

One day I was outside playing handball. One of the Muslim dudes that was locked up for the 1993 World Trade Center bombing plot was throwing the basketball at a window, trying to get someone's attention. The ball came on the handball court, and I told the guy to chill. It happened again, and I pulled him to the side and told him that I would beat his ass if I fell over the basketball. It took me approaching him in that manner for him to stop. I knew he didn't respect or like me because I was Black and American. Although I didn't have a lot of hate in me, I still had to work through the anger I was dealing with. Sometimes it got the best of me.

One of the dark sides to this prison was that I was around so many gangs and racists. There were skinheads, Mexican Mafia, Crips, Bloods, and many other gangs. They were all segregated. I've always been proud to be a Black man, but being in that prison helped me to realize how much some white people and Latinos really hate Black people. Everyone in that prison stuck to their own little clique. If you wandered off and were caught somewhere, some of the haters might try their hand and harm you. If you had a confrontation with the wrong person, then the consequences could be deadly. The guards' job was to monitor the activities of the prison, but ultimately it was up to us, the inmates, to protect ourselves.

My past experiences in prison made me not trust anyone while I was in ADX. Up to that point, all the facilities I had been to were state and private prisons. Being in a federal prison was different. I was around people from different states, cultures, and mindsets. I immediately began working out more. I had to be prepared for whatever. I was getting my mind and body ready for war. A lot of inmates there didn't like me because I'm a very outspoken person. That's just how I've always been. It's very hard for me to bite my tongue.

But my days of wreaking havoc and causing problems were behind me. I had changed. Prison wore me out. I'd grown up. I was a man, and I wanted something different for myself. I wasn't going to let anything get in my way of going home, but I also would not allow them to be disrespectful in any way.

I heard a lot of stories about guys called the cowboys, who mostly worked in the penitentiary next door to where I was. A lot of them got caught up in a corruption scandal, so they were moved to ADX, where their actions continued. These were correctional officers who were racist, and it was their job to demean and degrade us. They put feces in people's food, watched fights instead of breaking them up, and used violence as a means of intimidation. The staff played a lot of mind games in the ADX. They put me through a lot just to get my mail, money, and phone time. They did things in a certain manner just to let me know they were in control and that what I wanted meant nothing to them. Some days I was denied my phone call, or they wouldn't give me my mail when it came in. As much as they tried to get a reaction out of me, I remained cool. I read more books and did everything I was supposed to do.

During my time there, I was locked down a few times, but never for anything I'd done personally. Being locked down for twenty-three or twenty-four hours per day really took its toll on me, and each year felt like two or three years in solitary confinement. It made me appreciate life so much. It was tough because it tested my faith. As much as I wanted to give up and question God, I never did. I put in one hundred and ten percent to make it through my time at the ADX Supermax. I was determined to get out of there and make it home.

I also met a lot of good people; they were decent guys who tried to get educated and do what it took to better themselves. I met a few dudes from DC, and we made a pact that we would get our GEDs. I took a lot of different classes to keep busy. The classes included Counseling, Intro to Personality, Parenting, Domestic Violence, Drug Education, Coping Skills, World History, Africana Studies and many more. These classes really helped me because they raised my awareness about a lot of different issues. I enjoyed learning and increasing my knowledge, unlike when I was a kid struggling with dyslexia. Going to these classes made me wiser, stronger, and gave me something positive to do with my time.

The program was only supposed to be three years, but unfortunately, I was in there for six years, even though I had no write-ups. ADX taught me how to exercise patience. I had no other choice. No matter how much I wanted to go home, there was nothing I could do to be released earlier. I had to wait. Imagine being told that you'd receive something you really wanted, and then on that day you're told you must wait three more years to get it. It was a tough pill to swallow. I knew that was all a part of the mind games being played by the prison system. They wanted me to stay longer to see if I'd get in trouble, but I didn't.

Finally, in 2005, after five years, I went to see the parole board. I was thirty years old. Those people literally had my life in their hands, and I was excited and nervous at the same time. I sat before a black lady and poured my heart out to her. I showed her all my certificates from the classes that I'd taken. I explained to her that I hadn't been written up in over seven years and that getting my freedom back was very important to me. I let her know that I had been doing what I was supposed to do and ultimately deserved the opportunity to go back into society. She looked me straight in my eyes and told me that she believed me. She said that she realized I'd been out of trouble, programming and doing what I needed to do to make changes in my life. It really meant a lot that she acknowledged what I was going through and what I was trying to accomplish as far as getting my freedom back. That nice lady granted me parole.

But I still had to sit around and wait for the parole commission to write me back with final confirmation. The letter came, and the news wasn't good. The commission decided to revoke my parole. I was crushed. That hurt me badly. I'd worked so hard to stay out of trouble. Yet they said that my level of violence was too high. They didn't think that I deserved to get out early. I couldn't understand how the lady granted me parole, and then it was snatched back by the commission. I was disappointed, but I also knew that I would be released in August 2006. That was my mandatory release date. That's the only thing I had to look forward to. I had to snap out of that period of frustration and realize that I had to stay safe, alive and out of trouble for one year.

In December 2005, I lost my Uncle Toney, and that hurt me so much because he meant a lot to me. If I had gotten parole, then I would have been there to see him before he passed on. My uncle's death really devastated me! During that time, I leaned on the strength of my ancestors. I thought about how hard they had to fight for freedom. I told myself that I couldn't give up and that I had to continue chasing my dream of being free again.

Solitary
—————— Confinement

I will never quite know the full effect that being in solitary confinement had on my mind, body, and spirit. I was in prison for fifteen years, and two-thirds of my time was served in solitary confinement. Being locked down in a small room all alone really took its toll on me. No matter how strong you may think you are, those walls will begin to close in on you, and you will not be your normal self. I've witnessed many men lose their minds behind those walls of hell. I didn't want that to happen to me. But it was very hard to prevent it from happening.

I was on lockdown on many different levels. From the lowest level of solitary confinement to the highest allowed in U.S. prisons. It is only by the grace of God and support from my family and friends that I made it through. Willpower, faith, hope and inner strength helped me to persevere as well.

If you have never been incarcerated, I want you to lock yourself in your bathroom for twenty-four hours and see how it feels. This was my life for over ten years. I slept, ate, and disposed of my bodily waste all in one room. After a while I had to find something to do with myself. Time goes by slowly when you're in that cell all alone. No matter how much I worked out, wrote letters, and read books, I still seemed to have a lot of time not doing anything.

I never thought that there would be a time in my life when I'd begin to talk to myself. Well, that's exactly what I began doing in solitary confinement. I often hallucinated and held conversations with myself. In some ways it helped with passing time, but in other ways it made me feel crazy. When the walls begin to close in, you will try to make sense of what's going on. That's just how brutal confinement is. I've witnessed many people try to take their life when in confinement. Some of them took sharp objects, cut themselves, and tried to bleed out. A few were successful.

I was in solitary confinement in DC Jail, Lorton, Red Onion, and the Northeast Correctional Prison (CCA). My time added up in all those places doesn't compare to the mentally straining six years I spent at the ADX Supermax. The operations of the facility itself and the staff made sure to let me know that I wouldn't have control over much. Although I knew that I couldn't control how the prison operated, I made sure to focus on the things that I could control. These were things like my workout regimen, thinking positive thoughts, spirituality, and increasing my knowledge through reading.

While in confinement, there were many days that I felt anger, sadness, frustration and guilt. Sitting in that cell caused my mind to wander, and I often thought about the past, present, and future. That caused reality to slap me in the face hard. My past was not pretty. I took someone's life. My present state was bleak. I was locked down in a 7x12-foot cell alone. My future was dim. I still had many years left in prison.

The only defense mechanism I had in prison was to think about the fun I had as a kid. I often thought about the times I went to camp, played football for the Boys and Girls club, did fishing, and the good times I had with my family. I went to jail when I was sixteen, so the only life I knew before then was my childhood. I had no other memories. If I'd only thought about being in prison I believe that I would've absolutely gone crazy.

When you're in prison for as long as I was, you begin to wonder if you'll ever be free again. These thoughts can be very harmful if you start to believe them. I always believed that I would come home one day. Although things got very dark at times, I never lost faith. I don't believe that my codefendant and I were bad kids, but we got caught up in the negativity that was around us. After years behind bars, I met a lot of good people. I also began to mature and grow into a man. Over time I began to take responsibility for my actions. To this day, I wish that the person who died had lived.

Lewisburg
———— Penitentiary

In July 2006, I was sent to the Lewisburg Penitentiary in Lewisburg, PA. The maximum-security unit is known for its culture of violence and is one of the deadliest places to do time in America. When I arrived, I was immediately placed in the hole with two other inmates. There were two beds and one mattress on the floor. I had never been in a situation like that before. I'd been in lockdown for the past ten years in a cell by myself, and then I was thrown in a cell with two individuals I didn't even know. Being in that arrangement was very difficult. Fortunately, they were good dudes, and there were no problems.

Tim was from DC, and Twin was from somewhere down south. On the first day I was there, we talked about the prisons we came from, how long we'd been locked up and just regular small talk. During that conversation, I found out that Twin was associated with a gang, and that made my antennas go up. Hanging around gang members could be dangerous because of the negativity that surrounds them. On the other hand, Tim and I spoke about DC; he was from a neighborhood right down the street from me. We knew many of the same people, but that really didn't mean much to me. I still had to keep my guard up.

Gangs were a very big problem in this prison. I wasn't a part of any gang and never wanted to be, so I never had an issue as far as that was concerned. However, I was bothered by the fact that I had roommates. After being in solitary for so many years, I had become stuck in my ways and had a routine. For a while I couldn't sleep, and every move my roommates made woke me up. Things could have gone a totally different way if I didn't fight hard enough to work through the transition. Many roommates got into fights, and there had been many deaths because of disagreements. But I wasn't going to let anything get in the way of my freedom. I knew that going home was closer than ever.

The first few nights, my roommates woke up and saw me walking around. They would ask me if I was okay, and I would tell them that I was struggling. "Jail is jail," Twin said one night. "No matter where you are and who you're with."

I looked at him with a confused and angry look on my face. He didn't understand what I was going through. I stopped walking and told them about me being on lockdown for all those years and that being in the cell with them was very stressful. I tried to work through it the best way that I could.

"E, just hold on," Tim said. "We are not a threat to you in any way, and we hope that you don't go the fuck off in this cell."

I just nodded my head. "I'm alright." But I really wasn't. I was going crazy with those strangers around me.

Lewisburg did have its bright spots. It was cool because I could go outside even though I was in the hole. Every day I was walked out to a cage that sat off to the side of the compound. There were five or six other guys in the cage as well. I'd always watch the guys on the compound and wish that I was able to walk around as freely as they were. I often saw people from my past and would holler over to the compound to say what's up. It was a great feeling because I hadn't been in population for about ten years. I was finally able to see people and communicate with them, although limited by the cage. When some of my guys found out that I was in the hole and would be able to walk the compound soon, they came near the cage and showed me some love. Even though they were about thirty yards away, it still felt good to see some familiar faces. I hadn't seen a lot of those guys in over ten years. KP came to holler at me, as well as Fats, Mark, and Damon, to name a few.

One week after I arrived, I was able to go into the compound and walk around for the first time in ten years. It was refreshing. I was able to feel the grass in my fingers, and I could walk around and feel somewhat free, even though I was in prison! The first day they let me out, I just walked around and enjoyed the sights. At times I became emotional because I wasn't locked in that cage anymore. I walked around and watched the basketball games, the baseball games, card games, etc. I sat down and talked with my friends and caught up on what was going on in prison and on the streets. I felt as if I were one step closer to my goal of freedom. It wasn't until then that I realized I had made it out of one of the world's most secure prisons, ADX. Not only had I made it out, but I was sane. I was still dealing with some issues, but for the most part, I was in my right mind.

Psychologically, I had to adjust. I had to adjust to the cells opening and people walking by so fast. I had to get used to seeing knives again because it had been a while since I'd seen and needed one. I had to walk to the chow, and I had to shower with others again. These were things that I couldn't do at ADX. There was a lot I had to deal with. I had to learn the lay of the land when it came to the people as far as friends or foes. I didn't know who to talk to and who to stay away from. It was crazy because people were walking all around me. The things that wouldn't bother a person normally were a problem for me. I had to get used to being near people again. I also had to get used to talking to people again.

Socially, I was uncomfortable and paranoid. I didn't want anyone close to me, and I didn't trust anyone. When I was in lockdown, I communicated with people, but most of the time it was through the vents, toilets, notes and yelling through the door. However, being up close and personal was a different form of communication for me. I felt tight and wound up. At times I felt myself feeling very aggressive for no reason at all. Being around others is what I wanted, but I didn't know the psychological struggles that I would be up against. My head was always on a swivel, and my eyes were on alert. A lot of the anxiety was the effect of being in solitary confinement for so long. But the other part I had to deal with was the fact that I was back in population. I had to adapt and make sure I stayed alive.

While in Lewisburg, I saw a lot of old friends that I hadn't seen in years, and I embraced them. I even saw some of the guys who'd turned on me when I told them I wanted to change my life around, but there were no hard feelings. I met one guy by the name of Dee, who was sentenced to 600 years. He was locked up for a few murders, robberies, and kidnapping. I read his sentence computation paper, and it said he'd remain behind bars until he was deceased. I brought it to his attention and told him the paper said, "You are here until you are deceased." I told him he needed to tell someone and get it changed. He told me that it wasn't a mistake and that he had indeed been sentenced to 600 years. The way he acted really caught me by surprise. He was very calm and mellow. He didn't show signs of frustration either. Most people with that amount of time felt like they had nothing to lose and wreaked havoc in prison. He showed me that not all guys with a lot of time were out of control as they are stereotyped.

I came across a lot of guys who wanted to do positive things and still take care of their families even though they were locked up. I met guys who looked forward to working just to send money home to their kids. An old man named Mike worked in the welding shop and made it his business to send his daughter money faithfully. He'd been in prison so long that he earned enough money to do so. He'd been locked up for twenty-eight years. He told me that he'd been sending money home for over twenty years, and that made him proud. I gained a lot of respect for him because, even at a low point in his life, he tried to do what he could for his family.

People played many different roles in prison. There were inmates who helped guys with their cases as if they were lawyers. I met guys who tutored and mentored other people as well. There was an older homie by the name of Bill who was good with law. He helped folks with prison write-ups and legal work such as appeals and time reduction. Another guy named Bobby was very smart and loved helping people in the education department. He helped people get their GED and other certificates. By that time, I'd begun to see life through a different lens. I was done with negativity. I only wanted to surround myself with positive, like-minded individuals.

While at ADX, I tried to get my GED but didn't accomplish it. I failed the math portion of the test twice. The last time I took it, I fell short by one point. I was so upset and disappoint-ed. Passing that test was one of my top priorities when I got to Lewisburg. I got a math book and learned how to do algebra and geometry on my own. I studied every day. I was eager to accomplish the goal of getting my GED. I knew that once I got back into society, having that would be beneficial for me in getting a job and beginning a new life for myself.

In the meantime, I also started playing basketball and lift-ing weights again. I joined the team for my dorm, which was called J-Block, and we were pretty good. We were one of the best teams in the prison. We only lost one game during the season. In jail there's a lot of sadness, but we found ways to have fun. Those are the times I really enjoyed. People often use the slogan – pay your debt to society – and that is what I did as an inmate. It was done physically, mentally, and spiritually. I paid my debt with my life.

I took up welding until it was time for me to leave. As my release date got closer, I grew more and more anxious. I tried to do my time and stay out of people's business because

I wanted to go home alive and not in a box. I didn't want to catch any more charges. I wanted my freedom back. About a week or so before I was due to go home, I was called to take the math portion of the GED. I prayed that I would pass, I studied hard, and I did end up getting my GED.

The day before my release I went to R&D to check in my property. I was happy and nervous at the same time. There was so much running through my mind because the day had finally come. I'd waited for it for fifteen years! I started to feel guilty that I was going home, and many good men would still be stuck behind bars. I was very nervous because I didn't know what to expect when my feet hit the ground. I thought about hugging my mom, brothers, grandmothers, cousins, uncles, aunts, and friends.

PART
three

Freedom

Then the day finally came. It was August 24, 2006. A CO came to my cell and told me to get my things together for my release. I was in such a rush to get out of there. I left a lot of shoes, stamps, food and things like that behind for some good men. I was called back to R&D in the early morning and waited for about an hour before my brother Eric and his friend came. I walked to the back gate, and it seemed so unreal. I felt like I was in a movie. There were a lot of emotions going through me. The guard asked me to state my name, date of birth, and a bunch of other things.

Next, he congratulated me and said he hoped that he'd never see me again. I was listening to him, but at the same time I was anxious and trying to hurry up and get out of there before they said it was all a mistake. I got to the gate and saw my brother sitting down on the curb. When those gates opened, a wave of emotions came over me. I was happy, sad, and excited all at the same time. I was happy that I was free, sad that I was leaving behind some good people, and excited to see how the outside had evolved. I hugged everyone and was overwhelmed with joy. I was finally free. As we walked to the car, I thought about the day the gun went off, my trial, being in the hole going crazy and the manslaughter charge in Ohio. I cried tears of joy as we pulled off.

After all the emotions wore off, the only thing that I could think about was getting some food – like French fries, fried fish or chicken. I wanted some bubble gum as well. I told my brother to stop and get some gum because I hadn't had any in years. We saw a gas station on the side of the road, and I told my brother to stop there. We pulled into the gas station, and I jumped out so fast. I was anxious to get my hands on some snacks. I hurried into the store, and my brother was laughing.

"Slow down, Slim," he said. "The store isn't going anywhere." I just laughed and continued to grab everything in sight. I bought gum, candy, chips, and a lot of other snacks.

At the time, I felt like a kid in a candy store because I wanted everything. I was so happy to be able to walk into that gas station and buy what I wanted. It felt good to just breathe good fresh air outside the confines of a prison. The ride back was about three and a half hours, and I remember just staring out of the window, reminiscing. I talked with my brother about what had been going on with family and friends. He told me that Steven was a mailman, Ju should be coming back out soon, and about the new babies in the family, including my nephew, his son, who would soon be born – a few days late.

When we got back to the city, I had to turn myself into 500 Indiana Avenue, where I had to take a urine test. I was trying to find out all I could while I was down there because the parole thing was new to me, and I needed to know who my probation officer was.

The secretary for the probation folks told me that I needed to go check in at Hope Village halfway house, so we drove there. While we drove over there, I looked over my release papers again, and there was nothing in them about me being in a halfway house. The plans didn't go how I had envisioned them because when we got to Hope Village, I was told that they didn't have a file on me and that I needed to go back and speak with my parole officer.

Once we left there, I asked my brother to drive through the neighborhood where I was born because it wasn't too far away from the halfway house. I wanted to ride down Stanton Road to see how the neighborhood looked. Little did I know those homes had been torn down, and there was nothing there but dirt. I couldn't believe that they were building new homes.

So we headed back up to Indiana Avenue. Once we arrived, I turned in my paperwork, took a urinalysis and handled a few other things. Then I just sat there and waited for a while. I grew frustrated. My brother needed to leave because he was on a time schedule. His girlfriend was in the hospital and about to deliver my nephew at any moment.

Finally, two community supervision officers came to get me. They walked up to me and introduced themselves. "Hello, my name is Ms. Thomas," one of them said. The other officer said his name was Mr. Wilson. "Mr. Ellis, your next step is to go to the RSC Center." Ms. Thomas said.

"What is RSC, and why do I need to go there?" I asked them. "My paperwork says I was to go from prison straight back into the community."

"The RSC is a twenty-eight-day program," she said. "And you have to go."

I told them that I didn't want to go to that place, but I wanted to start my transition off on the right foot. Even though I knew that I could have denied it, I didn't. The two probation officers were just doing what they were told to do, and I didn't want to make an issue for them. They explained to me that I was going to a twenty-eight-day inpatient substance abuse program. I told them that I didn't have a drug problem, and that I didn't need to be there. They told me that the DC parole division wanted people who had been in prison for a while to go to the RSC to slow down the re-entry process. The goal was to help figure out what's needed to decrease recidivism. I listened to them, but I honestly didn't know what re-entry or recidivism was at that time.

The lady and my parole officer took me to the RSC and checked me in. I didn't want to be in the program. It was almost like I had to reset my mind to even agree to go in there. I had convinced myself that I would be going right home to be with my family. Instead, I was being sent to a twenty-eight-day program. I wasn't talking too much as we rode over there because I was very upset, and I didn't want to take my anger out on the messengers.

The program is run by Court Services & Offender Supervision Agency (CSOSA). I thought the facility was nice because it was clean and seemed to be new. It stood about six to seven stories high, but the food was nasty, just like in all the other facilities I'd been in. They didn't put any salt or sugar in the food. To be honest, I would have rather eaten the food that they served in prison. Staying at the RSC was difficult for me because my expectation was to come home and spend time with my family. Instead, I was locked up for another twenty-eight days. I found myself starting to shut down because I didn't want to be in that place. I had to get used to the young guys playing, complaining, and some of the counselors talking to people like they were children. I had to show them that everyone in the program was not alike. The sad thing was some of them looked down on folks who were drug addicts and spoke to them like they were subhuman. Yet these were counselors who were being paid to help people.

While there, I bumped into a guy named Roach that I had been in prison with. He'd done eighteen or nineteen years. He gave me the rundown about the program. He told me all the things that weren't allowed and told me to watch my attitude. He knew that I used to be a hot head. I took his advice to heart and followed all the rules. Roach went into prison back in the late 80s for murder, and he was in Lorton at a time when it was crazy for real. He was a respected man in prison and held his own.

At the RSC, I sat in group therapy with drug addicts for three to four hours a day. Although I didn't want to be there, I was still touched by a lot of things that I heard. There were some sad stories. All throughout my stay in prison I had never had a drug problem, but being in those groups taught me a lot. There were some guys who had been on drugs for twenty-five years but claimed they didn't have a habit. They were in denial. Some dudes smoked PCP, hallucinated and did some of the craziest stuff you'd ever heard. Guys who were on crack talked about how they stole from their mothers to support their habit.

Listening to these guys really humbled me in the aspect of asking myself if I was in denial about what I needed to do for myself. I looked at the guys and thought to myself those guys are clearly in denial about being addicts. Am I in denial about anything? It made me sit down and talk to myself about the things I wanted for myself. Counseling was one of the things that I knew I needed, but I didn't want group therapy. I preferred one-on-one counseling because it was more personal and basically about my struggles.

Even though I was very upset with what some of the counselors were doing, I still showed love and respect to those who were battling addiction because I didn't think they wanted to be addicts. They fell prey to drugs, and some weren't strong enough to get help before it was too late. I thought about the people in the program and how I would want someone to treat my family members who dealt with addiction. It made me respect them for who they were and, at the same time, disagree with some of their actions.

While in the program I was given a psychological evaluation. Some of the symptoms I was diagnosed with were post-traumatic stress disorder, post-incarceration syndrome, and narcissism. They told me I was a narcissist, but I didn't agree with that. During the assessment, I stressed to the psychologist that I really love and think the world of myself. I think she took it the wrong way and believed I was conceited or too into myself, which was not the case. I am a humble person who would do anything to help someone in need. I am not selfish, and I don't think the world revolves around me. The doctor seemed like she didn't want me to love myself because I'd just gotten home from prison. Some people believe that we don't love or care about ourselves, and that's far from the truth for most of us. I think this lady had a real problem with me describing self-love to her. For some reason it was very hard for her to get it through her mind that people who come out of prison can love themselves. She spoke to me about how we made bad choices, hurt other people, took from other people, etc. I had to let her know that there are folks out there who had never been to jail or prison and who've made bad choices. I wanted her to understand that people are still people regardless of their past and the choices they make.

However, I do agree with the PTSD diagnosis because I've gone through a lot of traumatic events in my life. Incarceration is one of the most traumatic and stressful situations that a person can go through, so I really understood the PTSD diagnosis. PTSD is a mental health condition that develops after a person has gone through a terrifying event. It causes a person to have disturbing thoughts, flashbacks, nightmares, and anxiety about the traumatic event. I feel like going to prison was traumatic, but what is equally difficult is I must live with the fact that I took someone's life. I had nightmares about the incident for many years. I've thought about that tragic night a lot. I had flashbacks about my friend's grandmother being killed in front of me, seeing my best friend being taken on a gurney when I was ten years old, and about other things I saw and did in the streets.

One of the symptoms of PTSD is that a person seems detached from family and friends. I felt this way upon arriving home. I was used to being alone in a cell for so long that my social skills were gone. I was paranoid, irritated, and always had my guard up. I couldn't seem to just relax and enjoy life. I also had severe mood swings. One moment I felt okay, and then suddenly, I'd become angry. No one understood why I acted that way, and at the time I didn't either.

I also agree with the diagnosis of Post-Incarceration Syndrome. I'd just spent the last fifteen years of my life in prison. Many people who are in prison or have come home from prison have also been diagnosed with PISD. This is a mental health condition that is caused by prolonged periods of incarceration in environments that are punitive. In addition, there are very few opportunities for education, job training, and rehabilitation in these environments. It is most common in people like me who were in solitary confinement for consecutive years. Some of the symptoms include antisocial behavior, substance abuse, headaches, and memory loss.

Research shows that prolonged solitary confinement causes the brain to shrink, and that affects a person's ability to control their emotions and remember things. The lack of physical interaction with the outside world, lack of social interaction, and inability to do normal things is shown to put massive stress on the brain. There are many rehabilitation programs for PTSD and PISD. Talking to a therapist really helped me work through a lot of the issues I had, and I have always encouraged others to seek professional support after all we have been through.

After leaving the RSC, I was placed in a transitional home in northeast DC. It served its purpose as it helped me to slowly ease back into society. The only difficult part was that it didn't garner any job leads. Unfortunately, I felt like society turned its back on me and other formerly incarcerated. Although we'd committed crimes in our pasts, we should still be given the opportunity to work and provide for our families. I felt like I had paid my debt to society, but when I came home, I was still limited in what I could do. Plus, the programs I came across when I arrived home were terrible. Either they were overcrowded, or they just didn't have the resources to get me the help I needed.

It was discouraging to me because when I was in prison, I often thought about getting a job and earning money to take care of myself. I applied for some jobs and was told that I didn't have enough experience. Others told me that they couldn't hire me because of my record, and then I just didn't hear back from a lot of employers. The obstacles that I faced were what made me want to speak out and advocate for people who are incarcerated and returning citizens. I decided that I would get involved and be proactive in trying to make the proper people aware that there need to be better programs offered.

The day I walked out of the transitional house after ninety days was one of the best days of my life. I was finally a free man. I no longer had to worry about waking up early in the morning, and I didn't have to worry about meeting my curfew at night. I gathered all my belongings and went to my mother's house. I really can't put into words how excited I was. While I waited outside for the cab, I talked with some of the men who were in the program with me. I told them to stay focused and get their lives back on track. I gave some of my clothes away to a few of the men who needed some help. It made me feel good being able to help them out.

The cab finally pulled up, and I said my goodbyes to everyone. As I rode home, I just sat in silence. When I pulled up, I thanked the cab driver and gave him his fare and a tip. I immediately went in and hugged my mother and brothers. I was so happy to be with them in the house and not behind bars. I was overwhelmed with emotions to the point that I felt drained. All I wanted to do was talk with them and eat some good food. My mother cooked some salmon, rice, cabbage, and cornbread, and it was just like old times again. On that night I just lay in my bed and thanked God. It felt like old times being in my mom's home, smelling her cooking, and seeing her beautiful smile. As for my brothers, it was a good feeling being around them as well. I'd missed most of their childhood, and finally I was able to be the big brother that I always wanted to be.

Despite all the joy I felt, I soon realized I had to overcome a lot of adversity. Imagine being taken out of society from the age of sixteen to thirty-one. It's probably hard to even fathom that reality. It was mine for fifteen years, and I realized it more when I saw the streets of DC. During that time a lot of things had changed, and I had to quickly adapt to society. It was almost as if I had been put into a time capsule, and everything had been fast-forwarded. There were new buildings, stores, and condominiums being built everywhere. Another thing I noticed was that there were white people all over the city. In 1991, before I went to prison, DC was still chocolate city and predominantly black. When I came home, white people had taken over the city. Back in the day, if a white person was walking down the street after dark, there was a good chance that they'd get robbed. Now they walked their dogs and strolled through the city at any time of the night.

The streets felt congested as well. There was too much traffic, and everything just seemed to be moving extremely fast. It was not the DC that I remembered. I guess I was just accustomed to being in prison. Prison days go by slowly. They were especially long for me because I was locked down twenty-three to twenty-four hours a day for so many years.

One of the biggest challenges was that I had to learn how to catch the subway. Washington, DC is a heavily populated city, and many people use public transportation to come into the city to work. People come from Maryland, Virginia, and as far away as Delaware. On top of that, there are so many different trains. There's a green line train, red line, orange, blue, and yellow. One wrong move, and I could end up in Virginia, on the other side of DC, or somewhere in Maryland.

Probation

Although I was free from prison, I still had obligations as it related to probation. My probation officer, Mr. Wilson, was very respectful to me from day one, and he gave me all the support I needed. On my first day in his office, we talked about what I wanted to do with my life, my work experiences, my support group, etc. Then we talked about my past charges and my experiences in prison. I asked him about the urine test I was required to take, and he told me that I had to report twice a month for it and twice a month just to talk with him. He was nice enough to allow me to do both on the same day, so that saved me two trips per month. He informed me that he had a job to protect the community, but he also told me that my success was very important to him.

While in his cubicle I heard his supervisor talking to someone in the background. In my mind I told myself that I needed to stay away from that lady. She had a tone in her voice that she was not to be played with. After about a thirty-minute visit, I got up to leave, and Mr. Wilson and I shook hands. As I walked out, I heard the supervisor yell out that she wanted to have a sit down with me the next time I was in the office. So much stuff went through my mind, but I just said okay and kept walking. On my way out, there were some guys in the waiting room talking about someone who had just been stepped back for getting high. In other words, he was taken back to jail for violating his probation. For me that was further confirmation that I had to stay away from anything that wasn't going to help me move forward with my life. I had no intentions of going back to the hell that I'd come from.

I went out the front door and onto the street. The sun hit my face, and it felt so good on my skin. Many people take the sun for granted. They don't appreciate its radiance. For some reason it didn't feel the same to me when I was in prison. Prison had a strange way of making everything feel dark and gloomy, even the sun. I caught a cab home from Union Station, which is just blocks from CSOSA. While taking the ride, I thought about how I didn't know how to use the train or bus like everyone else. I felt ashamed. But then, as the cab drove down Sheriff Road in Landover, MD, I saw the Redskins' football stadium (now currently named the Washington Commanders), FedEx Field, sitting up high. I told myself that one day I would go there to see my team play a game in real life. I went to R.F.K, the old stadium, when I was a kid. I went to see the Redskins play against the New York Giants. When I was locked up, I always told myself that I'd go to the new stadium as soon as I was able.

When I got home, the cab driver said that the fare was $25. I couldn't believe it was that high.

The next time I met Mr. Wilson, we talked about how it felt for me to be free and what I had been doing since my release date. We also set some goals; one of them was to find a job. I talked with him about my wanting to take my time and not rush anything, because I didn't want to go too fast and cause things to go wrong. My goals consisted of staying away from negativity, being on time for visits with him and urinalysis, and to talk to someone when I got frustrated.

I also had the opportunity to have a face to face conversation with Ms. Thomas, Mr. Wilson's supervisor. She asked me to come to her office before I left. I had no idea what she wanted, but I knew I had to meet her. Surprisingly, when I got in there, we had a really good conversation. I felt bad because I pre-judged her based on the stereotype that I had about probation officers. She was nothing like I thought she would be.

She was genuine when she asked me how I was doing and if I needed help with anything. She let me know that her team was there for support. I told her that I needed assistance in finding a job and that I was frustrated.

She asked me why I always had a serious look on my face and why I talked like I was angry. I explained to her that I'd just come home from doing fifteen years in prison and was still getting used to being free. I told her that I had a lot going on in my mind, and those things hadn't gone the way I'd hoped. I let her know that I was still trying to figure things out. She reiterated to me that Mr. Wilson and everyone on the team was there to support me and to let them know if there was anything that I needed. From that day forth I've held the utmost respect for Ms. Thomas and her team. They helped me so much when I first came home.

As time went on, Mr. Wilson kept seeing me get in and out of cabs when I visited the office. He asked me why I didn't catch the metro. I told him that cabs were easier for me, but he didn't let me get away with that answer. He knew something was wrong.

"Do you know how to use the metro system?" he asked.

"No, I don't," I said, looking away. I felt so ashamed because I was a thirty-one-year-old man who couldn't do something that junior high school kids had to do every day.

Mr. Wilson didn't have to, but he took the time and showed me how to navigate and use the metro system. For him and his guidance, I'm forever grateful. I saved so much money by not having to take cabs after that. To this day, the metro is my primary form of transportation.

The first time that I rode on the train by myself was a challenge, though. I was extremely paranoid. I was not used to people getting that close to me. I wasn't used to people touching me and being up in my personal space. It was frustrating because folks were just rude. In jail I didn't have to worry about that. There are times that I still turn around and face people because they are too close to me. I would rather look someone in their face than have my back turned to them. One day, shortly after coming home, I got on the subway, and it was crowded, so I jumped right back off. I wasn't in the mood for it. Sometimes I think I am claustrophobic. I will never be able to explain all the effects prison has on me, but paranoia is one of them.

When I came home, I really wanted to work, be responsible, independent, and earn a decent living. Unfortunately, I didn't get that opportunity when I came home. It was very frustrating. One situation was that I was offered a position with Home Depot, and I was so excited. Finally, I thought, I had the opportunity to move forward with my life. There was a seven-year background check that I was aware of and wasn't worried about because my charge was fifteen years old. They still denied me the job.

I had another job interview at a fitness gym. They told me I wasn't qualified to be a floor monitor. I couldn't believe it. The floor monitor was the person who walked around and observed the gym. It didn't take any certifications to be able to do this job. I was familiar with weight lifting and conditioning from being around weights in prison. I guess that wasn't enough because they hired an eighteen-year-old kid with no experience. After they turned me down, they told me he was more qualified than I was.

Those are just a couple of discouraging encounters that I had when I came home. Not being able to get a job really hurt my self-esteem, but I continued to push and didn't give up on myself. I eventually landed a job doing landscaping with my cousin, Adrian. When I came home, he was doing a lot of different things, and one day he spoke with me about the landscaping opportunity. I told him that I wanted to work with him, and the next week we started working together. It was far from my dream job, but it put a few dollars in my pocket. On top of that, it gave me a sense of pride and independence, which was something that I'd been seeking.

—— *the* Forgotten Souls

Many people think that we can't change, but anyone can if they put their mind, heart, and soul into it. As I look back at my life, I had a lot of ups and downs that changed me in big ways (without a Foe, a Soldier never knows his strength). It is through those changes that I have become a better and stronger person. (When the Mask Comes Off, Then What?) We as people will make some bad choices in life, but we must learn to grow from those experiences the best way that we can, because it's our experiences that make us stronger people.

I have seen many men grow within those walls (prison), and I've also witnessed many men fall prey to the system you call prison. The effects that it will have on them can never be weighed. We are all looked upon as unchangeable people despite how different we are. The labels that are placed on us will affect us for most of our lives, if not forever, even if we live a productive life from that point forward. I could never know the full effect that (prison) has on my life, i.e., mentally, physically and emotionally. I am certain, however, that I will experience those effects for the rest of my life. My fight will be a lifetime fight, and I understand that. Therefore, I'm going to do what I can to stay strong. The world has changed since 1991. I am not the sixteen-year-old that I used to be.

When we are locked up for whatever we did or didn't do, we are so-called "paying our debt to society." Once we are done with our prison term, society, for the most part, turns its back on us, and that's how we become the Forgotten Souls!!!! We are not all a lost cause despite what most people think and want to believe. There are a lot of us who were incarcerated who are now doing the right things in life, in the so-called "free world," and yet it's still hard to get a break.

The government should make more pre-release programs and provide other services to help us get our lives back on track. It really would be helpful and appreciated. I live my life like someone in a narcotics or alcoholics anonymous group day-by-day and one day at a time. The streets are right in my face each day that I wake up, and they are calling my name. I fight my fight every day in hopes that I have the strength to walk my walk and turn away from what I know is wrong.

The nightmare of prison that I lived in for the past fifteen years is a reality that walks with me every day. I try to leave my nightmare behind me and just move on with my life, but unfortunately, it's not that easy to do. What I lived and saw will always be a part of my memory.

I will tell you that there are a lot of good men and women in prison who made some bad choices in life. I've been around some men who I know didn't break the law, but because they are true to the code of the streets, they refused to rat. It is because of that they will never get out again.

I have come across some men who are very educated and talented in many ways. I'm not glorifying what they did or didn't do to find themselves in prison, but I am acknowledging how smart these men are and how some of them could make a difference in this world if given a chance.

I have come across men from all walks of life in the eleven prisons that I've been in since I was a juvenile, and I respect a lot of them for trying to change their bad ways and do good despite their situations. The people in the world (not all of them) don't see or won't allow themselves to believe that people in prison or who were released from prison can change. Fortunately, many of us have changed and will change as we continue to grow from our experiences. There isn't a guidebook out here that shows a person how to change their life around after doing time in prison or living the street life. It will be hard for many of us, but I'm here to say that, if given a chance to change, most of us will. However, I do believe that we must dig down deep within ourselves to find the strength to want to change and then seek the help needed for support, for we can't do it all by ourselves.

I believe that people who have been to prison are some of the strongest individuals in this world to be able to go through what we've been through. Not everyone who goes to prison will survive. Yet, despite my strength, prison has brought many negative effects on my life. I can't even get on a train, subway, or bus without feeling trapped and nervous. I also don't trust people like I once did. I honestly don't like this feeling at all, so I've decided to seek help. I understand that I can't fight these battles all by myself.

I really want to stress the fact that God was and is the key to my survival. The faith that I have in God has made a big difference in my life. In addition, I can't explain how vital my support group was for me when I was incarcerated. These people include my family, friends, and the positive people that I came across in my travels. Those people are just as important to me now that I'm free as when I was incarcerated.

Adjustments

There were a lot of adjustments that I had to make once I came home. One of the hardest adjustments that I had to make was learning about my family again. I was away for fifteen years and so much had changed for me and them. I had to sit down and talk with many of them about the new me and what I had gone through. Some of my family were interested in getting to know me, and others weren't. I don't know if this was because they didn't think it was important or if they just had no interest in getting to know me because of what I had done. In fifteen years, I'd grown from a sixteen-year-old boy to a thirty-one-year-old man. I saw life through a different set of eyes. I was mature and viewed myself in a more positive manner than when I was out in society as a kid. The prison experience allowed me to appreciate my life and freedom in a way that I'd never done. Most of all, it allowed me to focus on God and how most anything can be overcome with faith. I believed in God before going to prison, but going through what I went through showed me how important having a healthy relationship with God is. Coming home made me realize that God is real, and I believed he had great things in store for me. However, I still had to overcome some obstacles.

This was a very tumultuous time in my life, and everything seemed to be moving fast. Of course, I was happy to be free, but I was still dealing with a lot of wounds that prison had inflicted upon me. I had a lot of different stress factors to deal with. Getting reacquainted with family was a major one. The truth is that I didn't know them anymore, and they didn't really know me. My family couldn't understand why at times I would be so angry and frustrated. In many ways I was lost, caught up in a whirlwind. I was trying to move forward with my life, but in so many ways I couldn't. This caused me to lash out. One minute I would be fine and then, minutes later, I'd be extremely angry or sad. Those were the range of emotions that I'd deal with throughout the day. I tried to keep my hands busy by working out, playing ball, and working, but the frustration was still there.

Then I had an epiphany and realized that it was all a test. The devil was riding my back and waiting for me to slip up and send me back to a dark place. One day I was riding the subway and on my way to a job putting up sheetrock. I had my tool bag and in it was a pocket knife I used to cut holes in the drywall. I was so happy, and it felt good to be working. While getting off the subway a younger guy bumped into me. I turned around, and he was frowning at me. I grabbed his arm and said, "Hey, young man, I apologize for bumping into you." He looked at his friend and said, "See, I told you", as if to say he had punked me out.

It took a lot of restraint for me not to do something to that little guy. It really upset me because he really put himself out there and had no idea of what kind of situation, he could've gotten himself into. However, I used restraint, walked away, and went on with my day. The old me would've punched him in the face or done something that could've possibly landed me back in jail. It was then that I realized that God had changed my life.

I had another situation while working on an emergency clean-up crew with DC public schools. The foreman repeatedly kept raising his voice at me, which was a trigger. He reminded me of the prison guards who yelled and talked to inmates with no regard. On one occasion, I asked him to stop raising his voice and being so aggressive. He didn't like that. He said he could say whatever he wanted because he worked for the school and we didn't. I turned to walk away, and the foreman followed me. I turned, faced him, and told him that if he continued to follow me, I was going to kick his ass. He retreated. I was so upset with this guy that I tried to trick him into going to a part of the school where there weren't any cameras so that I could knock him out. He never followed me, and I am glad he didn't because it wouldn't have been worth it. It's so ironic because that day was the anniversary of my being home for a year, August 24, 2006. Two years later, I witnessed something I thought I'd never see in my lifetime. Barack Obama was elected as the first black president of the United States of America. The day before the election I was so nervous. I kept thinking that I would mess something up while casting my vote. I'd never voted on anything a day in my life up to that point. I really thought that they would turn me away and not let me vote. On this day I thought about all the time my friends and I sat around in prison and talked about one day being a part of society and being able to vote. It was around this time that I made the determination that I never wanted to bring harm to another person. I was so excited that I sat down and dedicated this piece to Barack Obama.

My First Vote

The year was 2008 when I first had the chance to vote. My voter number was 86. I'm very proud that I got the chance to vote and that history was made the year that I voted because Barack Obama became the President.

I wanted to see him win, and I made sure that I got up at five a.m. to get ready to vote because it was my very first time. It felt funny when I walked up to the school where I was to vote because I saw all the people standing outside getting ready to go in to cast their votes. I was hyped. The line was moving, and I looked around at all the people that were around me (all races of people). When I was allowed to go in to vote, I messed up on the first ballot, and I was afraid to ask for help and say that this was my first-time voting. However, I found the inner strength to ask for help, and I got another ballot and cast my vote. It felt so good.

When the day was coming for me to vote, I thought back to the history books that I had read and the old civil rights things that I saw in schools and on TV. It made me so proud to vote for the first time because my people fought and lost their lives for the next generation to have the right to vote.

When I used to read history books and see films on the civil rights movement, it always brought tears to my eyes or just made me upset because of what my people went through. I always wanted to fight back in some way because people fought for me and my generation. We need to understand for ourselves why voting is so important!

(Before I move on, I would like to thank the men and women who fought to allow me the chance to vote; Much honor!)

I feel that some people really take voting for granted and don't understand how important it is in so many ways. I was one of those people when I was in prison, but as I started to read more, my way of thinking really changed. I don't believe that Obama was perfect, and there were some things he did that I didn't agree with at times, but I feel that he was trying to do what was best. Nonetheless, I wanted to be out there to give my vote to the First Black President!

The day he won, tears came to my eyes because I was so happy to see a man of color become President. But the thing that I respected the most about him was that he was for people (all people). I couldn't predict then whether he would do a good job or a bad job, but at that moment I was just happy that he won. I liked what he stood for as a person.

I am grateful that he won, but he wouldn't be able to change what was done before him overnight. I believed that a lot of negativity would come his way because people would have high expectations for him to fix things. We must remember that these wrongs were done way before President Obama stepped into office.

The thing that was so funny to me was that the people that voted for him or against him voted for him or against him for a reason. A lot of white people were very afraid because they didn't want to see that change, and some black people didn't want to see him win because they were afraid he would be assassinated or that he might fail. The truth, as always, is, *"what's going to happen, will happen."*?

I want the men and women who are in prison to know that there is so much power in voting. That's one of the big reasons why the system doesn't want you to be able to vote while locked up. The vote of the incarcerated and convicted felons could change a lot. The government knows that. The process whereby some of us can get our voting rights back and others cannot, I believe is, a part of the power games that the system plays because they know those millions of votes would make a change.

When I was casting my vote, I was nervous and happy at the same time because it was history that was about to be made, and I was a part of that history. As I said before, I understood that President Obama couldn't change what was put there years before him, but I trusted that he would do his best.

I know a lot of people who don't vote, and I try to tell them how important voting can be and how it can affect their lives. It's just not about voting for the president, but we should also be voting for mayors, city council, congressmen, etc. These are the people who make decisions that have a very big effect on everyday life. Their decisions affect the schools that our kids go to, our community, health care, etc., and we need to know this! While I was in prison, I really didn't know how important those things were. When I found out, I wanted to get on top of it and cast my votes for the people I felt would be helpful.

During my journey there were so many times that I just wanted to give up. However, there was always something inside of me that wouldn't let me. I know that a lot of that willpower came from God.

Watching the election results was an exciting time, but that was also a rough year for me. In 2008, I had a seizure while riding in the car with Boo, my childhood friend. She immediately took me to the hospital, and I was diagnosed with epilepsy, which is a brain disorder that causes seizures. I was prescribed a medication called Keppra, but I've still had many seizures since that day. I remember that I went into a deep depression when I found out. I didn't know how to deal with the diagnosis or how it would affect my life from that day forward.

Some of the symptoms that I experience are memory loss, staring into space, and chronic headaches. I still don't know where the issue stems from, but I do remember a time when I was in CCA prison in Youngstown, Ohio and was beaten by several corrections officers. A few guys who witnessed the fight told me that I had a seizure while on the ground being beaten. Then, one day when I was in Lewisburg, a guy told me that I would often go into a daze in the middle of a conversation with him and then snap out of it like nothing happened. I didn't believe him until more and more people told me the same thing. I was never treated for epilepsy while in prison, and I had always wondered why I had bad headaches, felt sleepy, and forgot things.

Over the years, I learned how to manage my epilepsy as best as I could by changing the way that I ate and managing the emotions which affect my epilepsy better. I have learned how to stay away from so much negative news, people, etc., because those things can affect me. I also learned to meditate and relax. All these things have really helped me in the long run.

Advocacy

By the time I was released from prison, I knew that being an advocate for those who were incarcerated and others who would be coming home was what I wanted to be. Thus, I began getting involved in different activities in the community. One of the first opportunities that presented itself was when I was invited to be a part of a class of up-and-coming community supervision officers. The purpose of the training was to teach the officers how to communicate effectively with those who are returning to the community that would be on their caseload. The trainers who put the class together used me as a decoy. I came to the class dressed very sharply in business attire, and they didn't know who I was. They passed out my profile sheet along with my prison and street charges to all the community supervision officers. Then they asked them what they thought about the person's life they were reading about and how they would help him if he were on their caseload.

Some people said that I didn't deserve to be out on the street, while others said that I needed mental health counseling. One person stated that I needed drug rehab. A few people said that I needed to be monitored every day, while others said that they would do exactly what my probation officer did to help me. Everyone had their own opinion. There was a lot of constructive criticism, and I took it for what it was worth. After getting all the feedback, the trainers finally introduced me and told the trainees who I really was.

I stood up and said, "My name is Eddie Ellis. I went to jail at the age of sixteen and came home when I was thirty-one."

The looks on their faces were priceless. Some of them put their hands over their mouths, and others' jaws dropped. They apologized and asked me if they'd said anything offensive. I assured them that I hadn't taken offense, but then I spoke and let them know that returning citizens have feelings and are human beings as well. I told them we want to be respected just like they want to be respected. I encouraged them to show respect to people who return from prison and to not treat them as if they're worthless.

I told them that the piece of paper they read was indeed just that, a piece of paper. I wanted them to know that I have feelings, and that I feel the same hurt and pain that they feel. After I finished speaking, some of them asked me questions about how it felt to be free and how being in prison really affected me. I expressed to them that it felt good to be free, but I still struggled with anxiety, paranoia, and adjusting to society. They also asked what I thought about the psychological evaluation and the symptoms that I was diagnosed with. I appreciated that a few of the CSOs walked over and shook my hand and gave me resources about jobs and other services. It showed me that not all parole officers are the same.

For the most part, I think everyone walked away with a new perspective on returning citizens. That was my goal from the beginning. I wanted these individuals to understand that when a returning citizen walks into their office, they must understand they're dealing with a person who has feelings, a family, and a range of emotions. I wanted them to understand that they don't have to talk down on us or be nasty just because we've made some bad decisions in our lives. The reality is that everyone has made bad decisions, some more severe than others, but at the end of the day everyone deserves to be treated with respect and get a fair shake.

During the process I learned to truly respect parole officers. My parole officer, his supervisor and the entire team were good people and cared about how people on parole were being treated. Before that training I had a bad view of most parole officers. I didn't like them. I felt like they just wanted to mess up my life even more. On that day, I met a lot of positive people who were really trying to help people and genuinely cared about them. I really enjoyed that experience. It was a learning process for both the parole officers and me.

I really can say that God has blessed me in ways unimaginable since I've been home. I've been fortunate to do so many different things to help others and to be a catalyst for change. In 2008 I began creating manuals with resources for returning citizens to use when they arrived home. I also sent many into the jails and prisons. To this day I still cringe when I think about how lost I was when I was released. I felt like I was being pulled in so many directions but going nowhere fast.

The purpose of the guide was to provide some type of roadmap for returning citizens. It listed services that could help them in areas of need, such as housing, jobs, mental health counseling, transitional support, etc. I researched all the resources available in the Washington, DC, area and compiled them into a book I called the Window of Opportunity Pre-Release Handbook. My goal was to make sure that every returning citizen had one of these guides in their hand on the day they were released from prison. I sold many of these books, and I also gave a lot of them away. My goal wasn't to make a profit, but I wanted to fill a gap where I saw a need.

Word spread fast about the pre-release handbook, and people from all over the city were contacting me. I used social media as my main marketing tool, and one day received an unexpected email. The email was from a lady named Camille. She wanted to buy one of my books for a family friend. We met up, I sold her the book, and I didn't think I'd ever see her again. But I couldn't get her off my mind. She was so beautiful to me. One day I built up the courage to text her. I was nervous and didn't know if she would respond, but she did. I thanked her again for buying the book and told her how beautiful she was to me. She asked me if I remembered her from when we were younger, and I told her that I didn't. She told me that she lived in Silver Spring, MD, not too far from me when I lived there. I called one of my buddies that I grew up with, and that's when it all made sense. "Camille is the girl you used to chase behind when we were younger," he said. I just smiled. I had the biggest crush on her when we were kids.

I moved to Silver Spring in 1989, and I still remember the first time I laid eyes on Camille. She was the most beautiful girl I'd ever seen. She was very pretty and quiet. The first time I tried to talk to her was so funny because she was shy, and I was nervous, although she didn't know that I was. As time went on, I got more involved in the streets, and I saw Camille only occasionally. Whenever we crossed paths, I would have the biggest smile. I loved to see her pretty face and hear her talk. She had me mesmerized.

Camille and I talked on the phone and texted back and forth for a few weeks, and then I finally asked her out on a date. I was nervous and didn't know how she would respond. She said yes, and we ended up going out and had a great time. I courted her for a while. We went to movies, park events, concerts, and sometimes just hung out by the water and talked. She told me about her two kids, Jamiah and Jermaine. She let me know that her kids meant everything to her, and I respected that. I met them about a year after we started dating, and I loved the fact that she didn't rush me into meeting them. It showed me that she had character and that she was a respectable woman. She waited to see if there was something there between her and me before she got the kids involved. Everything was fine from the time that I met Jamiah and Jermaine. They were well-mannered, had great personalities, and were just all-around good kids.

As far as the guides go, I published them for several years, and then I noticed an alarming trend. There was a high turnover rate when it came to employees who work at non-profits and social services in general. Therefore, the information seemed to get outdated quickly. Another issue was that funding for a lot of programs was cut due to the lagging economy. Therefore, one month an agency might be up and running, and the next month be out of business. I didn't think it was fair to have these guides out with information that wasn't current, so I stopped printing them. However, I didn't let that deter me from my mission of helping others.

In 2008, I founded a non-profit organization called One by 1. It is a 501(C)3 organization that works with communities and partners to provide youth and adult support and resources. We also develop workshops, training, and mentoring services. One by 1 provides re-entry support services and programs to men, women and youths who are in prison or returning home from prison. We provide life skills workshops to help them develop the critical coping and decision-making skills they need to keep their lives on the right track.

Our mission is plain and simple. We want to build up youth and adults, reduce recidivism and keep our communities safe. Those are issues that I'm very passionate about and areas where I would like to see change take place. We also provide mentoring services and skill-based workshops designed to build youth self-esteem and confidence and to cultivate leadership skills and improve decision-making.

I started this organization because I feel that minority youth and adults are over-represented in the justice system. This stems from a failure of their communities to provide for them both before and after incarceration. According to the Census of Juveniles in Residential Placement, 79,165 of America's youth were held in juvenile placement facilities in 2010. More than six in ten of them were minorities. African-American youth are nearly five times as likely to be incarcerated as their white peers. Latino and American Indian youth are between two and three times as likely.

The stereotype is that our youth are making decisions

that lead to incarceration because their homes, schools, and neighborhoods are chaotic and unsafe. However, we believe that what they need is love, attention, discipline, control, and role-models. We strive to be that staple in the community that will prevent youth from being incarcerated and prevent those coming home from being rearrested. The harsh reality is that once released, two-thirds of returning citizens are rearrested within three years, and within five years about three-fourths are rearrested. Those numbers are astounding and the reason why I've dedicated my life to helping others.

One of the most rewarding aspects of One by 1 is the speaking engagements it allows me to be a part of. I've spoken at George Mason University, American University, University of Maryland, George Washington University, Marymount University, Georgetown University, Winston Salem State University, and in a death penalty class at Howard University. Other speaking engagements include Wilson High School, Bethesda Chevy Chase High School, Milton Hershey School, Potomac Job Corps, and countless conferences. I even spoke on the Steve Harvey Morning Radio Show. The speaking engagements have been a positive experience for me because I feel like I am teaching and helping people understand that individuals do change after making bad choices. Each event is unique and a new experience for me.

The blessing about One by 1 is that my childhood friend Kia helped me get it off the ground, and Camille helped me finish the paperwork. I love the work that we do. I don't have much financially to give back to society, but I feel God has blessed me with the opportunity to inspire others, and that's the joy that I get out of doing what I do. I can't give life back to the person I killed, but I can give back to the community and do what I can to help young people stay away from a life of crime. To me, that's honoring him and his family. I want to let youngsters know they can overcome, change their life, and make better choices. Our challenges and struggles make us who we are today. I respect and accept my past for what it is and understand that God has allowed me to change.

Looking Out *of the* Window

On November 16, 2009, I went back to Colorado to attend the National Legal Aid & Defender Association Annual Conference to present on three panels (Collateral Consequences and Re-entry, Walking in Your Client's Shoes, and Community First). When I was on the flight to Colorado, I laid back on the airplane and thought about my time in the ADX-Supermax prison in Florence, Colorado – from 2000 to 2006 – and I became upset. That place was very dehumanizing in so many ways. I was sent to the ADX Supermax prison just days before my twenty-fifth birthday. This was the prison where the former warden had coined the term 'Alcatraz of the Rockies,' a clean version of hell. All I knew was that it kept the sun from feeling real when it shined on my skin, and it made the rain and snow just seem fake for some reason.

I thought about my friends that were still in there, and I prayed that they get out of there sooner rather than later.

I looked out of the window while I was in the air and saw all the beautiful sights of Colorado, and it made me very sad. While I was in the ADX, I was around all of God's wonders, and I couldn't see any of them. So I told myself that when I landed, I would purposely go outside to see all that I could see.

When I got off the plane, I went outside to get a cab to take to the hotel. I looked up at the sky and at everything around me to take it all in. And when I got to the hotel and up to my room on the twenty-second floor, I looked out at the beautiful mountains in the background, and tears came to my eyes. At the age of sixteen, I made some bad choices and ended up in the ADX by the time I was twenty-five, where I couldn't see any of these beautiful sights. In no way am I saying that I was supposed to be able to see these sights, but it just felt good that I came back to Colorado for a good reason this time, and not as a prisoner!

I was able to learn a lot at this conference and connect with a lot of different people from different states. I was allowed to join NLADA last year because it is an organization that partners with many other organizations and individuals who are doing grassroots and nationwide work in communities, courtrooms, on Capitol Hill, etc. I am trying to give back as much as I can and network with others who are doing good work. NLADA allows me to do that and a lot more.

I didn't tell anyone how nervous I was going back to Colorado because I didn't think it was important, but it was an emotional event for me. No matter what, I was determined that I would allow my inner light to shine and not allow it to be covered up like it was when I was in the supermax prison for those six years.

I know that I made some bad choices in my life, and I take responsibility for my actions. I can't make up for lost time or for the past, but I can continue to give back and encourage others to do the same. We can't allow our charges to define us or hold us back; so again, reach within yourself and find that strength to grow, ask for forgiveness, change and move forward and allow your faith to lead you.

The ADX was a prison that made you understand that you were in prison in all its ways. I did my best to try and not allow the prison to destroy me, but it was only through the grace of God that it didn't harm me too much. I feel like the Man in the Iron Mask because he didn't allow the mask to wear him down or destroy him, just as I refused to allow prison/solitary confinement to destroy me. I do know it's only by the grace of God and the help and support of family that I made it, and I thank all of them.

—— Change *is* Possible

In April or May 2012, Camille told me she had something to tell me. I just looked at her trying to figure out what she was going to say. My mind was running, but then she grabbed my hand.

"Babe, I'm pregnant," she said. My mind stopped. I remember looking her up and down, trying to see if I could see a bulge in her belly. I was so surprised and happy. I grabbed her and gave her a big hug. I kissed her belly and while doing that, tears ran down my face! I was so overwhelmed.

"I am going to be a father. Wow me," I said.

"Babe, even though you have my kids, you are now going to be a biological father."

"Thank you, God," I said, looking up to the sky. I had been in Jamiah and Jermaine's life for several years by this time. Even though they were not my biological kids, I loved them like they were and would do whatever I could to help and protect them. The beautiful part is that they loved me back.

After what seemed like hours, we talked about how we would sit the kids down and talk with them. On that night, so many things ran through my mind. It was racing and going in so many directions. All those thoughts were positive except for one. I lost my father to gunfire when I was a baby, and I know how that has hurt me for most of my life. I laid in bed and thought of myself dying and not being there for my child. Those thoughts weighed on me heavily. I asked God to remove those thoughts from my mind.

The very next day we sat down and talked with the kids

about the pregnancy. Jamiah started crying and gave her mom a big hug. Jermaine smiled and said, "Congratulations, Mom and Mr. E." Jamiah gave me a hug, and Jermaine shook my hand. We answered questions about when the baby was expected, but at the time, we didn't know whether it would be a boy or girl. I was still living with my mother at the time, so we drove over to the house and gave my mother the news. She was so excited.

As days passed, I came down off cloud nine, but my mind was still all over the place. I didn't know what to do or feel, but I did know that I wanted to be alongside Camille every step of the way. Throughout Camille's pregnancy, I tried to make every doctor's appointment, because I wanted to make sure she and the baby were okay. I remember being so proud walking into the doctor's office with her. Camille helped me understand what was going on and why she had to go to the appointments.

After a few months we finally went to get a sonogram. I was eager to find out the sex of the baby and was wishing for a boy. I remember people told me that if I wished for a boy, then I was going to get a girl. I didn't believe in all that. But, regardless of what God gave me, I was going to love and protect my child the same way.

I sat nervously while in the doctor's office, waiting for the sonogram. Camille asked me if I was nervous. I looked at her and told a big lie.

"No," I said. "I'm good."

The nurse finally called us to the back, and my heart raced. The doctor talked to us for a few minutes and then put some gel on her belly. He rubbed this hand-held device on her stomach, and it looked like he was doing it with force. I asked Camille if it hurt, and she said no. About twenty minutes or so went by, and then the doctor looked over the pictures that came out.

"It's a boy," he said. I was smiling from ear to ear. I knew instantly that his name would be Eddie B. Ellis III. The doctor told us that the baby looked good and healthy.

Around the fifth or sixth month, we did a walk through at the hospital. The purpose was to help us be more prepared at delivery time. We walked through the different floors and passed the room where the babies are kept after birth. We also went into a delivery room, so we could see how that is set up. They talked to us about preparing a suitcase ahead of time and making sure a ride would be available. As the walkthrough was ending, the situation became more real to me. I was going to be a dad!

As her delivery date got closer, I thought about how I used to say I'd marry the woman who gave birth to my child. I believed that if you were good enough to have my child, then you were good enough to be my wife. I had previous relationships that didn't work out for various reasons. But I learned a lot from those situations. I always hinted at marriage to Camille, but didn't feel comfortable talking about it too much. I didn't know if that was what she wanted.

One day I threw a hint out there, and Camille asked what I meant.

"I want to marry you," I said.

"And I want to marry you. Let's do it," she said. This was another happy moment in my life, and I'll never forget that day.

I know that marriage is a process. Shortly after I proposed, I moved in with Camille and the kids. We wanted to get a feel for one another and what things would really be like living together. When people live apart the dynamics of the relationship are so different. We knew each other well, but we felt we needed to get to know each other on a totally different level.

Fortunately, everything went well, and we started ring shopping!

On December 31, 2012, Camille woke me up at about four a.m. and said that her water had broken. I was half asleep and

I said, "We need to turn it off."

"No, my water broke. The baby is coming."

My brain blanked, and all that hospital training went out the door. Camille told me to get the suitcase and to start the truck. I did that and ran back into the house. She was sitting on the bed breathing heavily. I gave her a pair of my sweatpants to put on and helped her up the stairs. I ran and told the kids and her mother, Ms. Blossom, what was going on. When I came back down, I told her I would drive, and she gave me a look like, "Are you crazy!" I didn't have a license and I have seizures, so she was not having it. We got into the truck with her behind the wheel and headed to the hospital.

When we got there, we walked into the emergency room and I told them that the baby was coming. They put Camille in a wheelchair and took her to the back to check her vitals. They hooked her up to different machines, and one of the nurses checked to see if she was dilating. After checking, she told us that Camille would give birth soon. Camille laid back on the bed. I grabbed her hand and asked God to protect her and our baby. I stared at her and started to cry because I was so overwhelmed. She looked so beautiful with a glow that I can't explain. I called my mother and told her, and she told me that she would come soon. We made a way for the kids and Ms. Blossom to get to the hospital, and we texted her sisters and nephew.

A few hours went by, and a doctor came and checked on Camille. I looked at Camille and could see that the baby was coming. The doctor wasn't paying attention.

"Doc, look what's going on," I said.

She turned around so calmly and said, "Okay, we got it." They went over to assist Camille, and then my gift from God came out. Tears rolled down my face because God blessed me with a child. I was so happy that I witnessed him come into the world – WOW!!

He didn't cry like I expected him to. He just looked around

the room at the faces. Camille held him so tight and looked up at me and said, "Here is our son!"

The nurses took Eddie to the scale and weighed him; he was six pounds, twelve ounces. They checked his eyes and his breathing. Then they took him to the nursery. I followed them to see where they were taking him. I was being protective already. I saw them place him in a little bed where the other babies were. I asked the nurse why he couldn't stay in the room with us, and she told me about the observation that they had to do.

I wasn't happy. I wanted him to be there with us. I just frowned and walked away. I went back into the room with Camille, her mother, sister, and the kids. My mother and brother were also there. We talked and laughed, but I was so tired. I looked at Camille and could see that she was tired after all her body had gone through. I never told her this, but I sent the word around that she had to get some sleep. Everyone stayed for a little while longer, but eventually people started to head out. I watched Camille close her eyes and fall asleep. I just wanted to sit there and protect her. I stayed up as long as I could, but I ended up falling asleep in a rocking chair.

For the next two days people came and went. We ate, played with Eddie, and I slept in the room and wouldn't go home until Camille and my baby came home. I washed up in the room every day. Many days we would sit in the room and just talk. Camille and I laughed about the day her water broke and how I reacted. I laughed about my state of confusion, but at the time, I really was lost.

When Eddie came into the world, I was looking to do some more work. I wanted to get out into the community and help more people. But I turned down a few offers because I wanted to be home with my son. I had some nice contract work that I was doing, so I was okay as far as money was concerned. I enjoyed the time I stayed home with Eddie. I changed, fed, and washed him. I played with him, walked him in the middle of the night to put him back to sleep, and went to his doctor appointments. I am a real hands-on father. I wanted to help Camille out as much as possible. Those moments are priceless.

The time finally came for us to go ring shopping again, and I was excited. After careful searching we found some that we really liked. That was a special day for me because I was finally able to put the ring on her finger. I was happy and blessed.

Throughout 2014 we talked and planned for our future together. We went to marriage counseling with Pastor Calvert and Rochell, who have been in my life for years. They went hard on us in the marriage counseling classes, and I am happy they did. It got us out of our comfort zone and made us talk, open up, and think more. I had done some immature things in my past, and I wanted to be a better man, person, and father.

I went into my marriage as a man who wanted to be married and have my own family. We asked Pastor Calvert if he would marry us, and he said yes. I was so happy because to have a friend I love as a brother seal the deal was an honor. Time went by fast. January 24, 2015, was the day Camille became Mrs. Ellis. I was so nervous on the day of the wedding. I was thinking about crazy stuff like, what if I trip while walking down the aisle? Or what if I freeze up while exchanging vows? I was a wreck.

On that morning, we woke up very excited. We ate, got everyone together, and headed to Patuxent Greens Golf Club. We got married at the beautiful Clubhouse Plus Scenic Course. When we got there, our family and friends were already there. We briefly greeted them and then headed to get dressed. I kissed Camille and told her that I loved her. "I love you too," she said. Camille and Jamiah went to the dressing room together. My mom took Eddie and Jermaine, and I went to another room to get dressed.

As I was getting dressed, Camille's godfather, Mr. Randolph, knocked on the door and asked if he could come in. He was like another father to her. He said that she looked extremely happy and told me that he was happy for us. I let him know that she spoke very highly of him and thanked him for being there for her on her big day Camille lost her father in 1996 and her godfather was like a brother to him. He talked about how he had watched her grow up and how glad he was that he would be able to walk her down the aisle.

After I put on my pants, shoes, and a tee shirt, I walked out to greet a few of the guests. While I was out there, I couldn't believe how nice the decorations around the venue looked. Camille's best friend Chantel did an amazing job as our wedding planner. One of the first things I noticed while walking around were framed pictures of both of our fathers surrounded by candles. Seeing my dad made me very emotional because I wished my father could have been there to support me and see my wife and kids.

I saw baby Eddie, and he ran up to me saying, "Daddy, Daddy." I picked him up, hugged him, and walked around to introduce him to people who had never met him.

As we walked I saw Josh, a younger brother and friend who worked as one of the administrative supporters in the probation office when I was on probation. He became like a little brother to me. We talked, and he played with little Eddie for a bit until I saw Janie. She is an elder that I met years ago doing advocacy work. She is one of my mentors and a dear friend. "I am so proud of you, Eddie," she said while hugging me.

As time went by, I grew more anxious, so I tried to sneak into the room to see Camille. "No," her friend Monique said. "You know that is not good luck, Eddie."

I just laughed and walked off. When I came out of the hallway, I saw Monique. Monique has been our biggest help and support with One by 1. I gave her a big hug and thanked her for coming. She is like a sister to us, and we are so proud of her. I also saw my father's twin, Willie. I was so happy to see him. We talked for a few minutes, and he picked up Eddie and gave him a big kiss. I asked him to hold Eddie for me because I had to head to the back to finish getting ready. I had thirty minutes to get myself together. I was so nervous!

As I was walking to the dressing room, Jermaine was coming out looking sharp. "You're looking pretty dapper in that tux," I told him.

"Thank you, Mr. E," he said while giving me dap. As I picked up my shirt, I thought about seeing Camille walk down the aisle. Tears came to my eyes, and I just smiled. I couldn't believe it. I was getting married.

Camille's godfather came to the door and asked if he could come into the room. "Man, it is packed out there," he said. "Everyone is excited and getting settled in." I reached for my tie, and that's when I realized I didn't know how to tie one. I asked Mr. Randolph if he could help me, and he did. I never liked wearing ties, but this day was special.

I walked out of the dressing room, down a hall, and into the room where the ceremony was held. As I walked in, all I saw were the smiling faces of family and friends. I walked around giving out hugs, thanked people for coming, and held small talk. My mother and mother-in-law told me how nice I looked and how happy they were for us.

My friend, Pastor Calvert Edison, asked people to sit and get ready for the ceremony to begin. I took my place up front in the wedding procession line while Jamiah, Jermaine, and Camille's Godfather took theirs. Jermaine, little Eddie, and Camille's mother walked in together. Jamiah and her godmother walked down the aisle next. I remember that the music was playing, and then the door opened. I saw my beautiful soon-to-be wife appear with her godfather. They walked down the aisle, and I felt like I was in a daze. I just stared at how beautiful she looked.

When they got close, I took her hand, and the Pastor started talking. He asked us to repeat what he said, and we did just that.

Then he asked, "Do you take this woman to be your lawfully wedded wife?"

"Yes, I do," I said.

Then he asked Camille, "Do you take this man to be your lawfully wedded husband?"

"I do."

The next thing I heard was, "You may kiss your bride." I did just that, and I couldn't hear anything around me. My heart was beating so fast. I was excited. I'd gotten married. We walked down the aisle and out into the other room, where we took our first dance.

After that, Camille and her godfather did the father–daughter dance; and then my mother and I did a mother–son dance. And then my wife and I danced to a few songs together. I honestly felt like I was floating on clouds. We looked into each other's eyes and started smiling. And then she laid her head on my shoulder and said, "Babe, we did it!"

Afterwards, we opened the floor for everyone to join us. People came to the floor, and we jammed and had a good time. I danced with my grandmother, and it was a beautiful feeling. I couldn't help but have tears in my eyes. There were so many emotions going through my mind. All of this felt like a dream or a book I read while in prison because, with all that I went through in life, things like this didn't happen to people like me. But this was real, and all I could think about was that CHANGE WAS POSSIBLE!

PART

four

Reflections

One day in 2019, my family and I took a day out to spend time at Hains Point Park in DC. As I sat there watching people in the park walk, ride their bikes, and fish, I just thanked God for all He had done for me. As the sun went down that day, the sky had a beautiful blue tone with a hint of orange. I looked over at my wife sitting in her chair and beside her, little Eddie playing with his Transformers and Black Panther toys. Jamiah was on her phone, and Jermaine had his headphones on, listening to music. I smiled at them and then asked my wife to come and hug me. I thanked her for never giving up on me – loving, supporting and encouraging me through the tough times.

"Of course, Babe. You are my husband. That's what I am supposed to do."

We talked about the work that I have done and the impact that I have had on the lives of others over the years. We didn't catch any fish this time, but I was overwhelmed with joy and glad to be around my family.

There have been so many good things that have happened to me in the last few years. I was hired by the Campaign for the Fair Sentencing of Youth (CFSY) on January 1, 2018. The mission of this organization is to lead and support campaigns to ban life without parole and other extreme sentences for children. In partnership with those directly impacted by these policies, we build coalitions, educate key decision-makers and influencers through the media and in-person meetings. We negotiate with key stakeholders and advance reforms that promote and ensure that people get a second chance.

I was hired as the coordinator of Incarcerated Children's Advocacy Network (ICAN). ICAN members are formerly incarcerated men and women who demonstrate through their advocacy that children, even those who have committed serious crimes when young, can mature and change. ICAN identifies, mobilizes, and amplifies the experiences of individuals incarcerated as youth to inform the public debate about children's capacity for positive change. A major goal of their advocacy is to debunk racially charged and dehumanizing narratives that seek to justify extreme sentencing of children.

I am very blessed to be able to work with so many passionate people who care about the people first and then the mission. I have the opportunity to talk about self-care with men and women who come home from prison and be connected to CFSY/ICAN. In 2018 we hosted our first self-care retreat in Scranton, PA. It was such a powerful retreat. We hosted eighteen former juvenile lifers from all over the U.S. They came to the retreat to learn more about themselves, to learn about being vulnerable, and about forgiveness and effective communication. I became an ICAN member in 2016, and I have met many ICAN members since who are doing amazing work in the community.

In 2019 this is the life that I live, and I want everyone reading this to know that Change Is Possible.

Advice for Young
—— People and Parents

When I speak to young people, I try to be mindful of the struggles that they go through. I try not to preach or speak down on them because I understand they are fighting an uphill battle. I remember back when I was a kid, people used to preach to me and talk down to me, so I wasn't very receptive to what they said. Their words went through one ear and out of the other. Some folks told me that I would never grow up to be anything, and, in the same breath, they'd tell me to do my best. I didn't understand and would shut those adults out. I believed they were negative and didn't have my best interest in mind.

Then, there were folks who told me to stay on the right path, to listen to my elders and stay in school. I learned to appreciate those people as I matured because I believe they wanted what was best for me. I believe that as adults, it's important that we build rapport with our youth and attempt to get an understanding of how they're really feeling and what they're going through. I don't think we should dismiss their feelings. We should help them deal with their anger, depression, and other issues. We should encourage them to talk about their problems.

We need to let our young men know that it's okay to cry sometimes, and it doesn't make you less of a person if you do. I also express to the young men that they are kings and princes, and they must honor themselves as such. I always tell young girls that they should love and respect themselves no matter what. I encourage them to not be caught up in materialistic things or looks. I let them know that they are beautiful princesses and queens, no matter what anyone says about them. I encourage them all to be leaders, not followers.

Peer pressure is a part of life that most kids go through, and it affects adults as well. I feel that it's important that parents tell their kids they don't need to be a part of a clique or a gang for them to feel important. Kids need to know that they are loved and wanted whether they are in the in-crowd or not. It really bothers me that many kids feel like being smart is not cool when in fact, being intelligent is something to be very proud of. These days our youth are ashamed to do things such as play chess, the violin or anything that stimulates their minds. I tell young people all the time that they should reach for the sky and think outside of the box. I tell them that they can be whatever they want to be, and it doesn't have to be a rapper, basketball player, or entertainer. I let them know that there are many career paths to choose from. However, I tell them that if they do decide to pursue one of those dreams, then be the best at it and never stop pursuing an education.

It's sad because a lot of young boys and girls are unsure and afraid of who they are. Parents should always tell their children they are special and that their future is very important. For the young people who are reading this and have been in trouble, it's never too late to turn your life around and make better decisions. You can't give up. If you do, then you've surrendered your true potential.

Never in a million years did I think I'd be where I am today, but I didn't give up. Even when I was in prison, I was determined to not come out and be the same person that I was before. I realized that change was possible. I believe that many of our young people are lost and misguided because parents don't pay enough attention or listen to them. I think a parent should pay attention to their child's habits, what they do and what they don't do, and what they are into. As adults, we should help them create a space where they can grow, learn, and feel loved.

For example, one day I went to a speaking engagement at a youth detention center for girls. A young lady stood up and stated that she wished her family would have listened to her when she was home, but no one would. She told the story of how the baby she conceived when she was fifteen years old was fathered by her uncle. She told us that she repeatedly told her mother and other family members that he was molesting her, yet no one listened. That caused her to lash out; thus, she got into trouble with the law. I say all of that to get the point across that listening to your child is an important aspect of parenting. Don't ever tune them out. The words that young girl spoke really brought tears to my eyes. No one listened to her, and when she acted out, she got in trouble. But that was the only way she knew how to deal with her pain. We must listen to our kids and the youth in the community. Sometimes their behaviors say a lot to us, and we miss the message.

If possible, try to keep your kids active in programs, sports, and whatever they have an interest in. Make sure they are doing something positive with their time. Kids get bored easily, and their minds will begin to wander. People often ask me how was it so easy for me to change. I tell them that it wasn't easy at all and that it took a lot of hard work. They say, well you make it look easy. I tell them I just do the things I feel I need to do to keep moving forward. I understand that it's not an easy task to change after living a certain way for so many years. After being in prison for so long I adapted to my surroundings, and the environment became a part of me. However, I learned to free myself of the negative behaviors that took place in prison. There are some lingering effects of being in prison that I believe will always be a part of me. Post Incarceration Syndrome, PTSD, and not fully trusting anyone are just a few. I will have to deal with those things, and I'm willing to do that, but I'm also ready for change.

Change must start with self. No matter what situation

you are in, you must find the strength to help change yourself. Realistically, some people have mental health problems
that won't allow them to change. Even with medication, life
is difficult for them, and they have a hard time adjusting. I
don't believe that the prison system itself is going to change
us, but we must do what we can to keep ourselves strong and
deal with our obstacles the best way we can. Sometimes the
obstacles are easy, and sometimes they are difficult. But either
way, you must strive to overcome them. No one can do it for
you. You must put in the work, time, and effort. If you need to
seek help and support, then go and get it because it's all about
enriching your life and future. Lean on your support group for
help, and don't be afraid to ask for it.

Advice *for* Incarcerated
— *and* Returning Citizens

Now, I want to talk about some steps that will help those who are still incarcerated. The first thing you must do is realize that you must be ready to change, and your transformation must begin while you are still in prison. The reason I say that is because when you come home, life is really going to start moving fast, and certain things will upset you. You may not be able to get a job immediately. You may not have any money, and your family may not be in a position to help you financially. There will be many obstacles to overcome. If you get angry and discouraged, then it's going to be difficult to make good decisions. If you're able to begin your transition while in prison, you'll already be accustomed to staying away from negative behaviors. Mentally prepare yourself for the struggle that lies ahead of you because once you come home, it will be easy to fall back into your old ways. However, if you're already disciplined in your new walk and have trained yourself, then you're ahead of the curve.

To be successful when you come home, you must have a strong support group. You should surround yourself with positive people who can help you live a productive life. I had my mother, brothers, my wife, my best friend, Boo, my probation officers, and other family members. You want to be around those who will steer you in the right direction and encourage you to stay away from negativity. You need to be around friends and family who are living the type of life you want to live. If your circle is full of people who have goals, dreams, and aspirations, then they will inspire you to have the same mindset even though you may have different goals, dreams, and aspirations. You want people in your corner who can genuinely help you. I'm not talking about financial help but people who you can call on when you simply need to talk.

It is very important that you take your parole seriously. When I came home, I was intent on completing all the guidelines of my probation with no infractions, and I did that successfully. One day I walked into Mrs. Roberts' office. She was my federal parole officer in Maryland. She told me that I was being released off parole, and it was deemed that I was not a danger to the community.

"Eddie, you're doing such a wonderful job," she said. "If there were more people like you, then I wouldn't have a job. And honestly, I would be okay with that."

"Thank you, Mrs. Roberts," I said with a nervous laugh. "I really do appreciate you. You encourage me, support me, and believe in me."

Tears began to roll down her face. At that point, I realized that she really did care about me. I hugged her, and then I became emotional. I thought about all my ups and downs and the fact that I never gave up on myself.

I was granted a release from all restrictions in 2010, three years earlier than my original release date/max date of 2013. That was a good feeling for me, and I advise people who come home to set a goal to not violate probation. My urine was never dirty because I don't use drugs, and I was always on time for appointments with my probation officer. I also took the initiative to get involved in programs in the community to help returning citizens. I wanted to lead by example, and I couldn't do that if I did something that landed me back in jail.

It turned out to be a blessing that I was sentenced under the Youth Rehabilitation Act when I was a teen. My case was sealed once I completed the terms of my parole. That made things a bit easier for me as I sought employment opportunities and didn't have to worry about being labeled a felon. I am grateful that I was given a second chance and happy to know that the program is still in place and other youth can benefit from it. Recently, there was a group of people who wanted to get rid of the YRA. They didn't feel that it was necessary. I had the opportunity to speak in front of some decision-makers about its importance and how it helped me. Fortunately, the YRA was held intact, and young people will continue to be able to have a second chance in life.

Lastly, another important thing to remember when coming home is to take care of your body. You can't be irresponsible when it comes to relationships, alcohol, and drugs. You must be conscious of the many diseases that people carry. There are a lot of individuals that you wouldn't suspect of having HIV and other sexually transmitted diseases. Those are things that you may have forgotten about while incarcerated. I know it's difficult after being locked up, and you just want to have sex. However, I just want to let brothers and sisters know that sex isn't worth losing your life over. You should protect yourselves and wear condoms. Not only that, but you should also be aware that you run the risk of bringing another life into this world. There is nothing wrong with wanting to have kids, but getting focused, finding work, and acclimating yourself with the outside world should be your priority.

For individuals with drug and alcohol problems, I believe you should seek treatment in the form of Narcotics Anonymous or Alcoholics Anonymous. There are a lot of free programs available, and you should take advantage of them. You can't be afraid to ask for help, and you must be ready to change. You must face the reality that you have an addiction, and it is hindering your life. I encourage you to stay away from people who engage in whatever your vice may be. Do your best to get clean before you come home. It's going to be ten times harder to stop using when you're back in society.

I don't know if a lot of you know, but there are many people out here in the community who feel that we (returning citizens) don't deserve a second chance or the opportunity to be helped. There are some people out here fighting for us, and I am very happy and thankful for their contributions. But some of us (returning citizens) must fight this fight also because it's our story and a part of our lives. We have a lot of knowledge to give and a lot of people to help. I wish that more returning citizens had the opportunity to be employed by the different agencies that assist us. Many times, we are a part of panels and discussions, and we give a lot of helpful information, but we are not allowed to be an integral part of the solution.

Advice *for* Families *of* Incarcerated

For those who have family members that are incarcerated, please do your best to support and encourage them. Trust me when I say that they need you more than you can imagine. If you're ever unsure of what you can do to assist someone locked up, I would say writing them a letter would mean the world to them. I can't tell you how excited I used to be when I got a letter from a friend or family member. That communication would really brighten my day. I believe that I speak for most people when I say it is one of the best feelings in the world.

Hopefully, the advocacy that I do will allow me to help a lot of young men and women get their lives on track and prevent them from going down the wrong path. I'd like to get the message out to everyone about my experience and transformation. It's not just my story but the story of many inner-city kids. In fact, it could be your story. Think about a time in your life when you may have broken the law and could've gone to jail or killed someone while driving drunk or under the influence.

My Mission *as an*
— Advocate *for* Change

Whenever I have the chance to speak to people about my life and the choices that I made, both good and bad, it really helps me out a lot. I've realized that it's not good to hold a lot of stuff inside; it's therapeutic to talk about my past. Students usually ask me all kinds of questions, and I answer them as best as I can. I always get letters from them telling me what they thought of my speech. I believe I have changed some minds when it comes to how some of them think about returning citizens. I want these students to know that people make bad choices. Some have gone to prison, and some haven't. We all go through ups and downs in life, and it's our choice to try and overcome the things we are going through. At the end of the day, that's what my story is about. I want to give students something they won't learn in a book. I always stress to them to pursue their education, make good decisions, and live a positive life.

Since I've been home, I've participated in and successfully fulfilled requirements for the following certifications, training programs, and workshops:

- "Building Healthy Communities," National Legal Aid & Defender Association (NLADA)

- "Emerging Leadership," NLADA

- "Community First: Client Leadership for Justice," NLADA

- "Certification in Peer Mentoring," Court Services & Offender Supervision Agency, (CSOSA)

- "Offender Employment Specialist Training," Court Services & Offender Supervision Agency, (CSOSA)

- "Faith Based Initiative Mentoring Certificate," Court Services & Offender Supervision Agency, (CSOSA)

- "Workshop on Intentionality in Public Life," Harwood Institute

- "Cultural Competency and Diversity Training for Job Specialists," Federal Bureau of Prisons

- "Cultural Competency and Diversity Training for Law Students," Georgetown University Law School

- "Walking in Your Client's Shoes Sensitivity Training," NLADA

- "Cultural Competency and Diversity Training for Social Workers," University of Maryland Baltimore

- And many more

I believe that educating oneself is key to change and is one of the reasons why I've strived to educate myself. The certifications, training, and workshops that I have attended help equip me with the skills that I need when I go out into the community and serve. I feel that we're never too old to learn, and I'll always seek opportunities that will help me become better at what I do.

I served on the executive committee of the National Alliance of Sentencing Advocates & Mitigation Specialists (NASAMS), as Co-Chair of the Criminal Justice Section of the American Bar Association (ABA), Re-Entry & Collateral Consequences Committee, as a fellow for criminal justice and disabilities. I was a part of a reentry think tank for a year. I had the opportunity to be a part of attorney & social worker client centered trainings, and professional trainings for probation officers. I'm Co-Director of Outreach and Member Services at the Campaign for the Fair Sentencing of Youth (CFSY) an advocacy organization fighting to ban life without parole for children (17 and younger) nationally.

When I speak in front of people, I don't know what they will ask, do, or say. I've never had a problem with speaking up for myself, so when I walk into a room, I am very confident in what I am about to do. In my heart, I feel like I am representing those who are still in prison, and that means a lot to me. The television prison shows don't depict the true stories of life in prison. They are grossly fabricated. I want to be a voice for the incarcerated and returning citizens. I bring this up because I have come across many people who have asked me questions based on what they saw on television, and I had to let them know that ninety percent of those things are staged and fake. There are a lot of men and women who will change and do better things with their lives when they get out, but there are also a lot of people who will change and do right while in prison. This is something that I feel isn't shown enough.

I have spoken on panels with judges, lawyers, probation officers, councilmen, and social workers, etc. I've realized that I must allow myself to learn from them and educate them on the plight of a returning citizen. Not all my speaking engagements have been pleasant, and I understand that is the nature of what I do. I've had to lay down the law at some events because I felt people on the outside looked at people returning home from prison as if we were nothing. There have even been times when people who have come out of prison talked negatively about those still in prison. I couldn't believe that just because they'd gotten their lives together, they'd forgotten about the time they were behind those bars dealing with their own demons. No matter how well we do once we're released, I believe we must remain humble and be open to helping others.

I've also gone to some programs to speak and saw people

who were locked up with me. They were so happy to see me doing positive things. It brought a lot of joy to my heart. I wanted them to feel that they could change themselves and do what I am doing or even better. I let them know that I don't allow my past to hold me back from what I want to do in life. When I go to speak, I don't glorify the things that I did in the past, and I don't make light of those things because that's not cool at all. We certainly can't help anyone if we are trying to brag or glorify what we used to do.

—— Fighting *the* Fight

I am one who believes that life is a fight, whether it's good or bad. When we experience something good or bad in life, we must learn to take something from each situation and apply it to our future. We have a choice in life to give up or fight in all situations. If we have faith in a higher power and willpower, it can help us fight the fight, and if you don't believe in a higher power or don't believe in yourself, most times you will give up.

I went through a lot in my forty-seven years of living. Some of the things I went through I didn't know if I would be able to deal with, but I did, and I have allowed myself to grow and learn from what I've gone through. I had a choice to give up when things were hard, but it wasn't in me to just give up on myself and my life. But I couldn't have done it alone.

I have heard the saying for years: "I am strong as a rock." But drops of water can break a rock over the years, and those drops of water are equal to stress when it comes to the mind. Stress can break a person if they allow it to build up. There were times when I was in prison that it really bothered me mentally, and I was sad, upset and some more shit. But I knew I couldn't give up because I didn't want to allow the prison system to destroy me like I'd seen it do to many others.

I had some good days in prison as well – when I read a book, wrote letters, talked with my family and friends on the phone, got visits and talked with some of my friends who were there with me. We made our time work for us. I believe that prison can be mind over matter most of the time, and if you learn how to accept that you are there, you can then learn ways to cope with the situation and fight it better.

When your mind is clouded, you can't fight a good fight. I used to allow my anger to get the best of me for years, and I really wasn't getting anywhere. So, after a while, I had to learn new ways to fight and mix them with the ways I already knew. When someone is in prison, they must find ways to keep themselves together mentally, spiritually, emotionally and physically because if they don't, that place will break them down.

For example, when I was in one of the prisons, I was trying to get my good time for something that I did in the education department, and I realized that if I fought them physically to get my "good time," I wouldn't get it. Instead, I would have good time taken from me if I decided to fight people with my hands. I learned how to file for my good time the proper way, and I received it and realized this is a form of fighting as well. I just want the men and women who are still incarcerated and on parole and/or probation to know that we still have rights, but we've got to learn how to fight different fights to help our-selves. This comes with age and the willingness to learn new things.

I can remember some old timers used to tell me to file for my good time, and I used to be like, "I'm not filing for nothing." I said to myself, I'm going to do this or do that, and I still didn't get my good time, so I said, why should I fight these people with my hands and still not get what I was fighting for (that's a dumb fight). So, over the years I learned to fight a different fight that ultimately helped me get what I was fighting for.

I recommend that you try to educate yourself as much as you can on as many different subjects as you can, because we are what we know in many ways, and we are what we do in many ways. I remember, at times, I used to be so upset about everything. I used to allow every little thing to bother me, but as time went on, I had to find ways to stop allowing every little thing bother me because it just didn't feel good. In those sit-uations, no matter where you are, you must try to think your way out of the situation before your feelings and emotions get the best of you.

I know that change doesn't come overnight, and it takes a lot to change and to see where you went wrong in your life. No matter what we do for someone, it's up to them at the end of the day to change and reach out for help. With that said, I am going to continue to fight for those who are not ready to change as well as those who are ready to change, because we can't just close the doors on them. Freedom is what you make it and what you feel about life. I say that because there are a lot of people who are mentally incarcerated and who have never been in prison before. I advise trying to free your mind in there because you can't fight the fight when you are both physically and mentally incarcerated.

I believe that the reputation of a man (person) can get lost, redefined or even created behind those walls as well as in the community. Right now, I want to deal with the prison setting because it's dear to my heart. When you're doing time, the kids and siblings of incarcerated men and women still need your help despite their situation, and you can still encourage them, support them and help them not make prison their fate. Unfortunately, men and women of color are going to prison at a high rate, and we must step up and try to help and not allow prison to be the reason why we don't reach out to our loved ones to keep them from ending up in prison. When I was still in prison, I had to accept my situation for what it was (I was locked up), but I could still write my younger brothers/cousins and encourage them to do the right things, such as going to school and educating themselves. I didn't want them to go to prison like me.

If we know that these young people look up to us, we need to guide them away from the wrong path with the knowledge that we've gained over the years, because it's our kids who are going to jail and our families that are being broken up. I am out here talking to a lot of young people who are on parole and/or probation, and I just might know some of these kids' parents, but I do what I do because I care. It kills me to keep seeing all these kids/people of color going to prison for whatever reason. I know I can't stop everyone from going to prison, but I will try my best. These people know that Eddie is being real with them, and that means a lot to me. I found the strength to want to change while in prison. It was a fight over the years, but I knew in my heart that I could learn from this situation and do a lot of good with my life experiences when I got out. I wanted to encourage the people who knew me while in prison to do better as well.

We don't know what we can deal with until we go through it, and that's a fight in itself. I know it's not easy to do time after giving the government fifteen years, but I urge you not to give up on life, yourself, or your loved ones. For those of you doing time with those that are incarcerated, please don't give up on your folks who are in prison because they need you to help them remain strong, to have hope and to feel like they have something to go home to.

the Chains That
———————— Held Me

The chains were made to keep you held down and locked up physically and mentally, and for years those physical chains wouldn't allow me to move. The chains that were on me were wearing me down physically, and I started to act out socially and emotionally. I would often get depressed, become angry, and at one point, I didn't care about anything. I'm here to tell you that I didn't like the feelings at all because I felt empty on the inside. I tried to fight every chance that I got. Then one day I realized that I had to fight the mental chains first, and then the physical chains would come off.

Personally, I decided to fight it because I love life, and I didn't want to give up. I started to fight the mental, emotional and spiritual fight, and the chains felt like they were starting to loosen up a little bit. From that point on, I stayed on that road which helped me survive in prison.

The change came. I turned my life around and learned to better myself, and then and only then did I see a way out of those physical chains. I stopped doing the wrong things, but I didn't change the people I was around, and things kept popping up in my life. I just didn't understand why these bad things kept happening.

I truly believe that many people want to change their lives and ways, but they don't change the most important things, which are: (1) staying away from the wrong people; (2) staying away from the wrong places and things. That's why things kept occurring in my life that weren't healthy.

When I realized that it was the people that I had around me, I had to do something about that and change that. It was hard to do because a lot of those people were my friends, but I had to make a choice which was either keep dealing with the wrong people and stay in prison for the rest of my life or fall back and find ways to tell them that I had to think about "self" first and do what was best for me.

I don't think that you have to be locked up to feel empty because people who were never in prison feel that way all the time. Some people have taken their own lives behind that feeling. Personally, I decided to fight it because I love life and I didn't want to give up.

I learned that you can't win a mental, emotional and spiritual fight in a physical way.

I will always be a fighter, and I fought then for my freedom and my life, and I made it through with the grace of GOD and the support of my loved ones. I want people to know that we all go through situations in our lives that are rough, but please know that you can work your way out of your obstacles if you try hard enough.

We wear chains on our minds in the community and don't even know it or realize these chains keep us from being all we can be. The sad part is that we pass these unseen chains on to our kids and them to their kids.

I saw my chains when I was in prison. Do you see yours? I think that we as people sometimes incarcerate ourselves when we tell ourselves that we can't do something even if we haven't tried whatever it is. When we do this, it can hold us back in life.

I personally believe that mental and emotional chains can have a stronger hold on you than physical chains can, because there are a lot of people walking around out here in the free world who are afraid to speak up or stand up. They won't allow themselves to remove the mental chains of fear, failure, etc.

I know that I am a returning citizen, but everybody that I walk by doesn't know that. If I put in my mind that everyone knows that I just came home, then it would keep me from going to look for work, from trying to meet new people, from trying to do new things, etc. Those fears are chains – mental chains that will hold me back. I can feel and see the effect that fifteen years of prison has had on me, and I still have some mental chains on me that I will have to work off through the years. I am willing to work them off because if I don't, those chains will drag me down. I did my time, and I am out in the free world trying to get my life back on track, and I know that there are some chains that I must get off me. Most men and women that do a lot of time in prison really don't realize that they are carrying around these same chains.

When someone is in prison they are dealing with a lot of different emotions like anger, depression, hate, lack of hope, etc.; at the end of the day, it's up to the person to find ways to grow, become a better person, and find faith, hope, strength and belief in a higher power and self.

Faith vs. —————— Daydreaming

When I was young, I used to hear older people talking about faith and saying that if you had faith, good things would happen for you if only you believed in God or a higher power. As a kid I tried to believe, but I didn't really know what faith was or how important it was to believe in a higher power. As I got older, I started to see how important faith and belief are to our lives. They provide us with the strength and will to live despite what we might face.

Throughout my years in prison, I can honestly tell you that I have never questioned God or ever gone a day without faith in my heart/head. I believe that faith, hope, and willpower go hand in hand, and I wanted to make it out of prison one day and live a better life. I didn't know if or when I would ever get out of prison because people die in prison all the time from many different things.

I am not trying to compare faith to daydreaming, but I am trying to show you how faith and daydreaming played a big role in my life while in prison. I used to let myself daydream about the fun times in my life as a kid and about things that I wanted to do and never got the chance to do; it really helped me out a lot. I can remember when I used to get the newspaper and daydream about the things I wanted to be, the food I wanted to eat, the kind of car I wanted, the job I wanted, etc., and when I did that, it allowed me to break out mentally. I dreamed of winning the power ball, building Boys & Girls clubs, building homes in the middle of the woods, having kids, etc. That was fun and important to me mentally when I look back. I believe that we have all dreamed about something in life, no matter if it was big or small. Daydreaming can be so much fun if you allow your mind to wander in the right places. I truly believe that daydreaming allowed me to not take prison too seriously because I knew that would've really destroyed my mind. The ADX Supermax prison was made to destroy the human mind, body and spirit, but by the grace of God, it didn't destroy me too much. Daydreaming was vital to my mental survival. When I allowed myself to daydream, it put my mind in a positive place, and I didn't feel like I was trapped in prison all the time; and, quite honestly, it helped.

I can say for myself that faith and daydreaming really helped me survive prison. Besides God and the love and support from my family and friends, I couldn't have survived and made it out of prison without this.

I wanted to make it out and be a better person, but I knew that my change had to start while I was still in prison, so I found ways to change, and it worked. I had to believe in God, have faith, hope, belief, willpower, and support from family and friends.

I truly believe that God/higher power is a key to our survival as a people, no matter what the situation is. My belief in God started before I went to prison, but while in prison, God, prayer, faith, hope and spirituality became more important to me than ever. Faith became key to me because I knew if I believed in what was right, good things would come to me. Hope was key as well, because if I hadn't hoped that things would get better, then I wouldn't have been able to think positively about my future.

I believe that belief, hope and faith all go together. I believed I would make it out, change my old ways, and help others.

Willpower is key when it comes to life because willpower is inner strength. Inner strength is like courage. It allows you to say no, to walk away and stand up for what you believe in. My willpower didn't allow me to give up on life, myself or the people I loved! Even when things don't look good, without willpower, courage, and inner strength, you will give up no matter what the situation is.

My family and friends played a big role in my survival in prison because of their love, support, encouragement, letters and phones calls . That helped me out so much, and I needed those things to survive. I thank them for all they have done for me throughout my life, especially while I was in prison.

My friends played a similar role in my life and my survival of prison by writing, offering love, support, and encourage-ment as well. However, it was my best friend that was and is like family to me because she was there for me in ways that other friends couldn't be. We were extremely close, given that we had known each other since we were kids. I thank every-one for their love and support!

The love my family and friends gave me throughout my life and time in prison meant so much to me. It really allowed me to give back love and keep love in my heart while I was in a dark place. It made me feel special to have people love me despite the bad choices that I made in my life.

I have gone through a lot in my life, starting from birth. First, I was born fighting against crib death, but by the grace of God, I am still here. I was lost in the streets and I made some bad choices as a sixteen-year-old child and someone lost their life while I was trying to protect myself. Through it all, I believed that God would allow me to be free again, and with my freedom, I wanted to help other people stay away from prison and change their ways.

I want people to know that individuals can change and that with the right support, anything is possible. I personal-ly believe that you must have a mental/spiritual connection to something other than man. It becomes a fight for some to believe that God would allow them to go through these dehumanizing situations. It's not until you mature that you understand that it's not God that put you/us there, but it was our actions that put us there. I believe that my own actions put me in prison, and God saved my life with His grace. I had to believe in Him, His power to change things, His love and His grace. Again, this can become a fight if you allow it to. I decided not to allow this to be one of my fights because I believe in God.

When things are going bad in your life, it can be hard to believe that a God would allow you to go through so much. So to some, it's easier not to believe in a God/Higher power. For me, God has always been real and a part of my life, even when I was doing wrong; therefore, I take responsibility for my own actions and try to move forward with my life.

When I came home in 2006, I didn't know what I was in for after being gone for fifteen years. I was afraid of the unknown that was before me, but I knew that I had to keep faith in God and believe that things would be okay. At the same time, I had to not only keep my dreams alive and dream big but reach for my goals and make them come true.

A dream can be just that, just a dream if you don't try to put the work in to make it come true. So, it is vital to reach for your goals and believe even when things are hard because God is there with you.

I didn't know that my family and friends had to have faith as well. I learned this as I got out of prison, but while I was in prison, I couldn't see it. When I learned that my loved ones went through so much, it really hurt me a lot, because I thought it was only me going through my situation. However, I am thankful to God for giving them the strength and faith to stand by me.

Over the years, I also thought about the family of the person who had lost his life, and I prayed for them and wished them the best.

We are made up of emotions and feelings, and we all will

have our times when we feel happy or sad. If you are sad, try to find a way to feel better and don't allow your anger or sadness to bring you down, because it can be controlling in a very bad way.

I still have my days and moments when I am down and depressed for many reasons, and sometimes I don't want to get out of bed or go to work. Then, I think back to when I was in prison and how I wanted to be home so bad and have a chance to work and just be able to walk around when I want to. With that in mind, I get up and hope I feel better. And I make sure that I have positive people around me as well because they are very important in our lives!

Life is life, no matter where you are or where you have been. We all must find something to live and fight for. I urge people to find something worth fighting for, stand firm and never forget to Day Dream!

—— Acknowledgements

Camille, you have brought so much joy to my life in more ways than one.

She has been such a blessing to me and to my family's life. She has helped me through so many things that I was dealing with over the years. I want to thank her for allowing me to be that special person in her life and for allowing me to stand by her side and deal with life. There have been good and bad times with her, but she has never left me. When a person goes through prison life, it affects them in so many ways. I can't explain everything, but at times I made it hard for her to understand me and what I was going through.

Camille – I know that I gave you a hard time over the years, but you stuck it out with me, and I love you dearly for that.

I think that it's only right to acknowledge the women in my life and the kids before I go down the line to thank the other people that have been here for me through this struggle. I want to give a shout-out to my step-kids, Jamiah and Jermaine, who are some very good young people. I love you and wish you well in everything you want to do with your lives. And on December 31, 2012, God brought Eddie B. Ellis, III into the world, and a light came into my life that I'd never seen before. I love this little guy so much.

I want to thank my mom Sheila first and foremost, for her love and support through all that I went through from birth until now. I want to thank my grandmothers, Ella Mae and Annette, who are so very different, yet the same, because they both loved me and supported me throughout my life. And to my grandfathers – Clarence Cherry and Moe Ellis (R.I.P.). I love you guys.

To my brothers Eric and Emmanuel, I want you to know that I love you so much. I still feel guilty for taking myself out of your lives, but I am here now. To all my cousins on both sides of the family, we have our own relationships, and I am thankful for all of you. To my aunts and uncles – thank you all for all that you were able to do for me when it comes to love and support. To all my friends I came across throughout my life, I want to thank those of you who stood by me, and to my childhood friend Kia (Boo) who was always there for me, and her sons, who are some very good young men. I was also blessed to find a brother from another mother – Dr. N. D'Angelo Lewis – who has supported me over the years in many ways. Rebecca Milliken, Troy, Pookie, K.V, Abdul L, Xavier, Eric, Donnell, Catherine, Marshan, Jody, Crystal, James, Lori, Lil John, Dee, James R., Darrick, Halim F., April, My ICAN/CFSY family etc.

I want to thank Professor Colman McCarthy for allowing me to come to his classes to speak to the students. Jamael, my brother and friend, thank you for sticking in there with me over the years to get this book completed. I want to thank your family for giving you the time to be a part of this project.

To my probation officers who helped me along the way and to my Doc (Sam) that I visited, who helped me get my mind together when I came out, thank you. To the brothers who are still behind those bars, and there are too many to name, but you know who you are, just keep your heads up. To the people that I lost – father (Eddie Sr.) first, whom I miss so much, my grandfathers Clarence Sr. & Moe, Mr. & Mrs. Robinson, Aunt Tina, Aunt Denise, Uncle Toney, Great Uncle Brown-Bey, friend Robert "Pee-Wee" Thomas, Edwin (Eddie) Ellis, my sister-in-law Carol, my beautiful mother-in-law Ms. Blossom and to the others that I lost along the way, see you on the other side.

I have been through so much in my life and I try to count my blessings, but I can't because God blesses us in ways we would never know. I just give thanks to God for all that He has done for my loved ones and me.

— About Atmosphere Press

Atmosphere Press is an independent, full-service publisher for excellent books in all genres and for all audiences. Learn more about what we do at atmospherepress.com. We encourage you to check out some of Atmosphere's latest releases, which are available at Amazon.com and via order from your local bookstore:

Finding Us, by Kristin Rehkamp

The Ideological and Political System of Banselism, by Royard Halmonet Vantion (Ancheng Wang)

Unconditional: Loving and Losing an Addict, by Lizzy and Adam

Telling Tales and Sharing Secrets, by Jackie Collins, Diana Kinared, and Sally Showalter

Nursing Homes: A Missionary's Journey Through Heaven's Waiting Room, by Tim Eatman Ph.D.

Timeline of Stars, by Joe Adcock

A Boy Who Loved Me, by Wilson Semitti

The Injustice in Justice, by Charmaine Loverin

Living in the Gray, by Katie Weber

Living with Veracity, Dying with Dignity, by Alison Clay-Duboff

Noah's Rejects, by Rob Kagan

A lot of Questions (with no answers)?, by Jordan Neben

Cowboy from Prague: An Immigrant's Pursuit of the American Dream, by Charles Ota Heller

Sleeping Under the Bridge, by Melissa Baker

The Only Prayer I Ever Have to Say Is Thank You, by M. Kaya Hill

Amygdala Blue, by Paul Lomax

About the Author

EDDIE B. ELLIS, JR., was born in Washington, D.C. As a 16-year-old child, Eddie was arrested for murder, but later found guilty on manslaughter and sentenced to 22 years in prison. After serving 15 years, ten of which were spent in solitary, Eddie was realeased on August 24, 2006. Since his release, Eddie has dedicated his life to being a part of creating change and peace in the community. Eddie demonstrates his commitment in multiple ways and across various platforms, including sharing his personal experiences, struggles, and growth. Eddie's transparency, passion, and powerful message on self-forgiveness and reconciliation show that personal responsibility and accountability are the starting points for real change for all people, not just those impacted by the system.

Eddie's journey on advocacy has spawned exponentially; he has worked on a variety of issues, including reentry, solitary confinement, and on behalf of people with disabilities who are in the system and coming home. He has served on the board of directors of a National League Aid organization, helping with client center training for lawyers, probation officers, and social workers. He is an advocate for those in the system, a mentor, and a motivational speaker. His lived experience as a formerly incarcerated person provides invaluable insight and depth into his work that allows him to connect with and engage the community he serves.

Eddie joined the Incarcerated Children's Advocacy Network (ICAN) in 2015, which is a family of adults from across the country with former life other extreme sentences from when they were children. ICAN is an unparalleled network that thrives on positivity whose members prioritize being a part of change taking place in their own communities and not giving up when struggling with the personal everyday challenges that life brings. The Campaign for the Fair Sentencing of Youth (CFSY) hired Eddie in 2018, and he started to support, advocate, and testify around policies to ban life without parole for children aged 17 and younger in the United States. Eddie is also a champion for self-care/community-care for those who are impacted by the criminal justice system.

Eddie is a very proud husband and father who loves creating multi-media art, fishing, dogs, sports, and spending quality time with his family and friends!

Made in the USA
Monee, IL
17 November 2024

70349348R00111